Wrestling with Romans

BOOKS BY JOHN A. T. ROBINSON
Published by The Westminster Press

Wrestling with Romans

The Body: A Study in Pauline Theology

Redating the New Testament

The Human Face of God

The Difference in Being a Christian Today

Christian Freedom in a Permissive Society

The New Reformation?

Christian Morals Today

Liturgy Coming to Life

Honest to God

On Being the Church in the World

Wrestling with Romans

BY

JOHN A. T. ROBINSON

THE WESTMINSTER PRESS

PHILADELPHIA

The text of *The New English Bible* is the copyright of the Delegates of the Oxford University Press and the Syndics of the Cambridge University Press, and is used by permission.

Published by The Westminster Press®

Philadelphia, Pennsylvania

PRINTED IN THE UNITED STATES OF AMERICA

9 8 7 6 5 4 3 2 1

Library of Congress Cataloging in Publication Data

Robinson, John Arthur Thomas, Bp., 1919–
  Wrestling with Romans.

  "The letter of Paul to the Romans": p.
  Bibliography: p.
  1. Bible. N. T. Romans — Criticism, interpretation, etc. I. Bible. N. T. Romans. English. New English. 1979. II. Title.
BS2665.2.R6   227'.1'077   79-11645
ISBN 0-664-24275-8

Contents

Preface

I have vowed never to write a biblical commentary. For in a commentary you have to say something on everything, whether you have anything to say or not. This is why most commentaries in my experience are duller than books written by the same persons, even on the same subject. Moreover I never find myself wanting to read a commentary through. I use them as reference books, though I tend to go to them with my own question about a passage, only to find so often that they never even ask it, let alone answer it. But they are indispensable quarries.

Yet I have sensed the lack of something between them and books designed for daily or group Bible study or for meditational reading. What I suspect the student or the educated layman most often needs who is prepared to wrestle with the message of a biblical writing is someone to lead him through it, drawing indeed upon the best that scholarship can bring to it, but offering a sort of conducted tour. Such a guide will set the historical context, draw attention to the points of interest and importance, and help him through the parts that are heavy going, so that he emerges, hopefully, with a sharpened appreciation of its contemporary relevance.

This is indeed the function of a good lecture-course. Yet outside a university or theological college these are seldom available and are in any case confined to the few who can physically get to them. Moreover they tend to be exam-orientated and too narrowly technical. But popular lectures on television, and indeed the whole development of the Open University, have shown that there is these days a much wider audience for communication at this level. Students too have got wise to the fact that some of this material is often more suited to their purposes than that of academics writing with one eye on their colleagues and their research reputation.

An obvious area for such a conducted tour is St Paul's epistle to the Romans. It is the 'heaviest' of all his writings. It is not easy for anyone to read on his own or even in a group. How many parish or even college study groups deliberately go for it? A vicar, a former pupil of mine who keeps up his reading far more than most, on whom I tried out the idea, confessed that he would tackle anything rather than Romans. For it is full of profound and sometimes tortuous argument. Yet on any reckoning it is one of the formative documents of the Christian religion. Indeed it is the presentation of the gospel *par excellence* for those of us who are still politically and ecclesiastically the children of that Roman world which Paul addressed, and it is in the West that its repercussions have most been felt. In fact there has hardly been a radical reforming of the Christian battle-line in the West which has not passed through and often begun from this epistle.

Consider, for instance, Augustine with his analysis of man and original sin, based on chapters 5 and 7 of this epistle; or Luther with his doctrine of justification by faith alone, based on chapters 3 and 4 of this epistle; or Calvin with his teaching of divine predestination, based on chapters 9 to 11 of this epistle; or Wesley with his gospel of grace abounding, based on chapters 6 and 8 of this epistle; or Barth with his insistence on the righteousness not of men but of God, based on chapters 1 and 2 of this epistle, and whose commentary in 1919, that 'bomb on the playground of the theologians' (Karl Adam), marked the beginning of the modern period in theology.

It has been my privilege in the fifties and again in the seventies to have been asked to take students through this epistle at Cambridge. Since the course is now what the shops would call a 'discontinued line', I thought I would try throwing it open to a wider audience, preserving something of the speaking style. I have not, as I would if I were essaying a commentary, attempted to cover everything or take into account all the relevant scholarship. There are many cruces of interpretation which do not materially affect the sense that I have deliberately skirted round – or simply indicated where the arguments can be pursued. Yet, as my title indicates, I have not shrunk from grappling with the hard issues. For Paul's meaning can often be wrested only from a detailed application to his text and from a study at some depth of his big words. I have not presupposed a knowledge of the Greek; yet I would think it a failure of communication if one did not try to help the reader to get from the passage what can only be appreciated by going to the original. In fact, though there is no substitute for learning the language properly I would judge that for most students this is a more fruitful expenditure of time and effort than acquiring that statutory smattering that can these days suffice even for an honours degree.

Yet I do not promise only blood, sweat and tears. On the contrary, the epistle to the Romans offers what Winston Churchill also called the sunlit uplands, indeed the very heights of Christian experience and theology. But to appreciate them one must be prepared to work at it. A church where this wrestling is not being seriously attempted, especially in the most educated generation of its history to date, will be impoverished in its capacity to transform the world rather than be conformed to it. 'I am not ashamed of the gospel' says Paul in this epistle. But there is mental as well as moral cowardice, a sheering off categories of thought, like those of justification and expiation, wrath and law, which are strange or even repellent to our world. Yet not to wrestle through them is to cut ourselves off from most of what makes Romans 8 perhaps the greatest chapter in the New Testament.

Some Commentaries

I have merely noted a selection of resource materials from different viewpoints to which I refer from time to time or which can serve as a follow-up for further study. I have often drawn on them without cluttering the text with acknowledgments and I apologise when I have unconsciously raided their riches. For the reader who wants a single 'best buy' I would recommend Dodd or Barrett.

W. Sanday and A. C. Headlam, *International Critical Commentary*, 1895.
Still a classic critical commentary on the Greek text.

J. Denney, *Expositor's Greek Testament*, 1908.
By a noted evangelical preacher and theologian.

K. Barth, 1919, English translation, 1933; shorter version, 1959.
A powerful theological exposition that introduced a new era.

C. H. Dodd, *Moffatt New Testament Commentary*, 1932; revised Fontana edition, 1959.
Still perhaps the clearest presentation of the meaning of Paul for today.

K. E. Kirk, *Clarendon Bible*, 1937.
Good for its long introductory section on 'the main ideas of the epistle'.

A. Nygren, 1944, English translation, 1952.
A forceful interpretation from a Swedish Lutheran viewpoint.

E. Brunner, 1948, English translation, 1959.
A popular presentation by a great Swiss doctrinal theologian.

C. K. Barrett, *Black's New Testament Commentaries*, 1957.
Clear and reliable exegesis by a front-rank New Testament scholar.

Some Commentaries

F. F. Bruce, *Tyndale Commentary*, 1963.
A sound popular commentary with a particularly useful introduction.

E. Best, *Cambridge Bible Commentary*, 1967.
A straightforward commentary on the NEB text, especially for schools.

M. Black, *New Century Bible*, 1973.
A condensed commentary with many references to further reading.

E. Käsemann, *Handbuch zum Neuen Testament*, 1973.
A major commentary by a German Protestant scholar, still being translated.

C. E. B. Cranfield, *International Critical Commentary*, new series, vol. 1, 1975; vol. 2, 1979.
The latest commentary on the Greek text.

Introduction

It will be well to start with some brief remarks of a historical and critical nature to set the context and clear the ground, so that in what follows we can concentrate on the content.

The author, occasion and date of the epistle are fortunately all beyond serious dispute. There is general agreement that it was written by the apostle Paul to Rome, almost certainly from Corinth (cf. 'Gaius my host', Rom. 16.23, with I Cor. 1.14), just as he leaves Achaia (the Roman province of Greece) for Jerusalem (Rom. 15.25) for the last time with the collection from the Gentile churches (Rom. 15.26–28; cf. Acts 20.2–3). The absolute date of writing depends on when Festus succeeded Felix as Procurator of Judaea (cf. Acts 24.27) and therefore when Paul arrived in Jerusalem, which is unfortunately still uncertain. But we can be pretty sure within a year or two either way, and in my book *Redating the New Testament* (1976, p. 55) I have argued for the early months of AD 57 as the most likely date of composition. Paul's intention is to go on to visit Rome afterwards (Rom. 15.28; Acts 19.21) but already he has fears for his success or even survival in Jerusalem (Rom. 15.30–32), and in fact he subsequently reached Rome only as a prisoner.

The letter is sent to prepare his way. He had long hoped to visit Rome (Rom. 1.10,13; 15.23), but his missionary policy had always kept him where no other evangelistic work had been done (15.20–22), and even now he intends only a fleeting visit *en route* for Spain (15.24, 28), which is really as much a holiday in the great city (15.32) as well as being perhaps a sort of mission to the Capital (1.11–15). But there is no doubt that to Paul the Roman citizen the imperial city exercised a great pull. 'What Rome meant then is almost beyond our comprehension. We must imagine as one all the capital cities of our own day together, from New York to London to Tokyo. He, the Jewish itinerant preacher, is to conquer Rome for Christ. By what means? By the message of a Galilean who was executed as a criminal!' (Brunner). Reading between the lines in 1.8–15 we may judge that his eagerness to declare the gospel 'even to you in Rome' comes as the climax of his missionary career: 'the universality of the gospel makes him desire to preach it in the universal city' (Sanday and Headlam).

But at this point we must note the only important critical issue that need bother us. In 1, 7 and 15 one Western manuscript (G) omits 'in Rome' both in its Greek and Latin text, and there are signs from patchy efforts at reintroducing it that it was originally absent from the predecessors of two other bilingual manuscripts (F and D). This is not sufficient to make us doubt that Paul originally wrote the words. It is in quite a different class from the omission of 'in Ephesus' in Eph. 1.1 (where it is left out by our earliest papyrus witness, 𝔓⁴⁶, and by the original hand of the two best and earliest codices, Sinaiticus and Vaticanus). But it is certainly not accidental in both places and versions and, taken together with the confusion at the end of the epistle, raises the question whether the letter did not at some point circulate in two editions or even to two churches. The evidence is set out in full in the commentaries. Important new evidence came to light in the discovery in 1935 of the Chester Beatty papyrus 𝔓⁴⁶, so it is best to read a discussion of the issues since then. There are two main problems.

1a. The placing of the doxology (16.25–27). (i) The best manuscripts put it where it stands in our Bibles at the end of chapter 16. (ii) The majority put it at the end of chapter 14. (iii) Some have it at both places. (iv) Some including the Greek side of F and G mentioned earlier and the second-century 'heretic' Marcion omit it altogether. (v) 𝔓⁴⁶ (from about AD 200) puts it at the end of chapter 15.

1b. The placing of the grace (16.20b). It is found either (i) here, as in the best manuscripts (including 𝔓⁴⁶) and in modern English translations; or (ii) as verse 24; or (iii) in both places, as in the Authorized Version; or (iv) after the doxology in verse 27.

2. The list of names in chapter 16. How is it that there are so many if the Apostle had never been there before? 'Had Paul's

friends migrated in a body to Rome?' (Dodd). Our suspicions are aroused since a number of those whom we know about already were last heard of at Ephesus. But a strong case can be made for Rome notwithstanding, and one small detail might point in that direction. In 16.13 we read: 'Give my greetings to Rufus, an outstanding follower of the Lord, and to his mother, whom I call mother too.' 'A Rufus is mentioned in Mark 15.21 as one of the sons of Simon of Cyrene.... He plays no part in Mark's story and must have been named only for identification. This means he must have been known in the church (probably Rome) for which the second Gospel was written' (Barrett). For what it is worth this would help to confirm Rome as the destination, though of course the name Rufus ('Redhead') is fairly common.

So what conclusion are we to draw from the confused evidence?

In the first place many would hold that on linguistic grounds the doxology (16.25–27) is sub-Pauline – an imitation of his style (certainly it is more like that of Ephesians and the Pastoral Epistles than that of the rest of Romans). Many have argued that it was originally composed, probably by disciples of Marcion, to round off chapter 14, at which point we are told by Origen that the epistle had been truncated by Marcion, who wished to sever Christianity from its Jewish roots. He also excised, for instance, 10.5–11.32, and he could well have objected to the concessions to Judaism made in 15.4 (the Old Testament was written for our instruction) and 15.8 (Christ became a servant of the Jewish people). Later, it is argued, it was transferred by scribes with the full text in front of them to its natural place at the end of the epistle.

But if Marcion cut the epistle short at the end of chapter 14, how much did he cut off – chapters 15 and 16 or simply chapter 15? The majority of commentators, both British and Continental (and it is an impressive consensus) argue for the original integrity of the whole epistle down to 16.23. That is to say, the list of names belongs to Rome. But there are other possibilities.

Kirk argues that the original letter was 1–15, under the

3

influence of the then newly-discovered $\mathfrak{P}^{46}$ which places the doxology there, and that this circulated with two endings, 16.1–23 and 16.25–27. The different variations arise from attempts to combine these two traditions.

T. W. Manson (in his *Studies in the Gospels and Epistles*, 1962) also thinks that 1–15 was the original letter to Rome, but that by the addition of a covering letter of greetings in 16.1–23, it was adapted by Paul for sending to Ephesus (though without bothering to alter the address or the proposed itinerary in chapters 1 and 15 – that is to say, with 'in Rome' still in, which is only omitted by Western manuscripts); while the shortest recension of all (1–14 and the omission of 'in Rome') was due to Marcion with his anti-Old Testament and anti-Roman bias. Manson argues that the discovery of $\mathfrak{P}^{46}$ has made all the difference, in that it gives the manuscript evidence needed for regarding chapter 16 as a separate letter. But of course this still does not prove that it was not addressed to Rome, which must be decided on other grounds.

John Knox ('A Note on the text of Romans', *New Testament Studies* 2, 1956, pp. 191–3) argues that the original letter was 1–14, without the words 'in Rome', and was a general letter to Gentile churches that Paul had not visited but over which he wished to assert his apostolic authority. The specific address 'in Rome' and chapter 15, with his proposed plans, was then added for Rome, while a letter of greetings (16.1–23) was added for Ephesus. Knox's argument is neater than Manson's which requires that even the Ephesians received a letter addressed to the Romans with the details of Paul's Spanish tour thrown in. But Knox's argument, as he admits, would really point to the original letter ending not at 14.23 but at 15.13, which is the natural and rounded close of the argument before the plans begin. The end of chapter 14 is no *ending*, it can only represent a point where the letter has been truncated. But for any closure at 15.13 there is no manuscript evidence whatever. Moreover, the only evidence for the omission of 'in Rome' and for stopping at the end of 14 is suspiciously secondary to be taken as an indication of how the epistle left the hand of Paul himself.

So we find Barrett, Black and Cranfield returning to the earlier position of Dodd and others, ignoring 𝔓⁴⁶ as eccentric and holding the original letter to be 1–16.23. This, it is agreed, was mutilated by Marcion, the doxology being added first to 1–14, and then transferred to the end of the full text. And on balance I think that this (the most conservative position) is the most probable. J. B. Lightfoot, in lectures given at Cambridge a hundred years ago of which I have my father's notes, held that Paul himself later in the west (at Rome?) added the doxology in his maturer style to re-use the material and give it wider circulation in an abridged form (1–14) as a circular letter (like Ephesians). There is no real evidence for this – at least we are told that Marcion cut it –but, like everything that Lightfoot did, it is worthy of respect.

But when all is said and done it makes little difference to the theological estimate of the epistle, though some to the situation in Rome to which Paul was writing. If chapter 16 is integral, he already had numerous contacts in the capital which he is clearly fostering over against his visit. These may have been due to the scattering of the Jews from Rome under the emperor Claudius, probably in AD 49 (Acts 18.2), who had begun to return after his death in 54, when Nero, his successor, showed himself favourable to the Jews. This certainly applies to his two chief contacts, Prisca and Aquila (16.3), if indeed they were now back in Rome. In any case, Paul's ideas could well have had a good influence in advance through converts of his like Epaenetus (16.5).

It is difficult to be certain of the past history of the church in Rome. The best account of it that I know is in George Edmundson's largely forgotten Bampton Lectures for 1913, *The Church in Rome in the First Century*. Paul addresses the church, doubtless with a due admixture of tact, as though it were an adult and established congregation from whom he expected to receive as much as he could hope to give (cf. 1.12; 15.14,24,32). At least two of its number (if chapter 16 is Roman), Andronicus and Junias (or Junia), can be described as being 'eminent among the apostles' and were Christians before Paul (16.7). Possibly they were even among the 'visitors from Rome' said to have been present at Pentecost (Acts 2.10). Suetonius, the Roman historian, tells us that the expulsion of Jews from Rome took place on account of constant tumults *impulsore Chresto*', which probably implies an active Christian presence and struggles between the old believers and the new at least by the 40s of the first century. Indeed, Eusebius, the church historian, quoting Papias's tradition puts Peter's first preaching mission to Rome in 42, and this I believe to be not at all impossible. Acts is entirely unhelpful. Its sole reference to the Christian presence in Rome is in 28.15, to 'the Christians there' who had had news of Paul's arrival and went out to meet him. But thereafter Paul is recounted as proceeding exactly as he did when he was first in the field – going to the local Jews and then to the Gentiles. He gives no suggestion that anyone had been there before him, which was clearly not the case.

It is most unlikely that the Roman church had any original apostolic foundation. It could have come into being as the result of travelling Christians like Andronicus and Junias, although it is not at all improbable that Peter had preached there and had later, as Edmundson argues, gone on to Rome from Corinth in 55, after the death of Claudius, to strengthen the church there and to appoint elders. He may well have had a hand in building it up into an organized church out of a number of missionary outposts and house churches, three of which are mentioned in the final chapter (16.5,14,15). There is a description by the fourth-century Roman called Ambrosiaster, which from the fact that it does not claim apostolic foundation for the see of Peter looks trustworthy. 'It is known that Jews lived in Rome in apostolic times, because they were subjects of the Roman Empire. Those of them who had become Christians passed on to the Romans the message that they should profess Christ and keep the law.... Without seeing displays of mighty works, or any one of the apostles, they accepted the faith of Christ, though with Jewish rites.' But clearly at some time they *did* see both Peter and Paul, who were later honoured as co-founders of the church and certainly died there.

Introduction

The composition of the Roman church is of some importance for the understanding of the epistle, though virtually all we know about it is derived from the letter itself. There is an interesting analysis of it by Lightfoot in an excursus on 'Caesar's Household' in his commentary on *Philippians*. Sociologically it was probably largely made up of freedmen and slaves, but by no means only the submerged tenth. 'The better sort of Greek and some oriental slaves would often be more highly educated and more refined in manners than their masters' (Sanday and Headlam). Some were householders and Prisca and Aquila were in business as tent-merchants. The reference in 16.10–11 to 'the household of Aristobulus' (possibly the grandson of Herod the Great and brother of Agrippa I) 'and my kinsman Herodian' would point to the staff of the best families. The appeal of the early Christians was probably to the same class as that of the Communists today – primarily to the skilled unions rather than to the unskilled. Certainly some intelligence would have been needed to cope with the epistle to the Romans! Religiously and racially it was clearly (like all the churches Paul had dealings with) a mixed congregation, with Jewish and Gentile Christians side by side. Sanday and Headlam work out the names in chapter 16 as roughly: Jew 8, Roman 4, Greek 10. In chapter 14 the weaker brother who is a vegetarian and sabbatarian is evidently the Jewish Christian. But the chapter is addressed to the Gentiles among his readers with the impression that they are the dominating element. In 11.13–14 he definitely says 'I am speaking to you Gentiles'; in 1.5–7 and 13–15 he includes the whole Roman church among the non-Jewish world and 'the rest of the Gentiles'; and in 15.14–16 he tactfully justifies his somewhat prescriptive language by reminding them that they come under his universal apostleship to the Gentiles.

Yet equally the whole epistle presupposes a Jewish, Old Testament and rabbinic background and would be unintelligible to those who knew nothing of it. In 7.1 he says distinctly, 'I am speaking to those who know the law'. But this does not necessarily refer to the Torah – the appeal is to the acquaintance with legal statute in general and the point he makes is equally true of

7

Jewish and Roman law. In 7.4–6 and 8.3–4 he presupposes that his readers have been 'under the law', but then so in a sense has the whole pre-Christian world (2.14–15). In 7.4 again they are 'my brothers', an expression he uses in 9.3 quite clearly of his fellow Jews by race, though there he makes it explicit by adding, 'my natural kinsfolk'. In 4.1 he speaks of 'Abraham, our ancestor in the natural line'; but in I Cor. 10.1 he had spoken to the dominantly Gentile congregation of Corinth of the Israelites as 'our ancestors'. Clearly at times he is speaking *ad hominem*, and his imaginary objector in chapters 2 and 3 and elsewhere is obviously a Jew, though at other points (e.g. in 6.1) he seems to be up against antinomian (Gentile) objections. In fact, many of his Gentile readers would have come to Christianity via Judaism, as God-fearers and proselytes, and would have had a double background.

There have been those who have believed that the Jew-Gentile issue was *the* occasion of writing and consequently that chapters 9–11 which concentrate on this are the centre of gravity of the epistle and the climax of its doctrinal section. But 9–11 certainly reads like an excursus, and could well, as Dodd suggests, have formed an existing sermon or tract of Paul's on the Jewish problem which he has adapted to the context of the epistle. The purpose of the epistle seems to be not to deal with anything particular in the local situation, to which anyhow Paul was strange, though 16.17–20 may refer to disputes he knew of in the Roman church, and which were to surface painfully with the impact of the Neronian persecution in 65 (cf. 1 Clement 5–6 and O. Cullmann, *Peter, Disciple, Apostle, Martyr*, 1953). Paul seems rather to be taking the time off to set down a considered statement of his gospel as he had come to understand it prior to embarking on a new stage of his missionary career. It represents his last and most mature writing as a free man. It is the summary of his message and the apologia of his methods which he felt it advisable to send ahead of him to prepare the way for his visit and to allay the suspicions which had no doubt reached Rome, as elsewhere, from his Jewish opponents. In 15.30 he ends by issuing an earnest appeal for their prayers and co-operation. His confidence is that when he comes he will come in the fullness of the blessing of Christ (15.29). Though he appears anxious not to intrude on other men's work, and though he tactfully proposes only a brief visit, his suggestion of being sped on his way to Spain (15.24) could well be a hint that he hopes to be sent on to Spain with their backing, as their 'missionary'. And this may be intended to ripen into a plan to make Rome the base of his operations for the western Mediterranean, as Antioch and Ephesus had in turn been for the eastern. In any case, much is going to depend upon the reception that he gets.

Finally, a word on the structure of the epistle. Perhaps the easiest way to picture the progress of the epistle is as though you were making a journey by canal across an isthmus. You could imagine the epistle going from Corinth to Rome across the isthmus of Corinth, though the first canal was not in fact begun until about ten years after Paul was writing. It was started by the emperor Nero in 66–67 with a work-force largely composed of indentured Jewish slaves, and then abandoned unfinished. Until that time smaller vessels were apparently dragged over bodily on some sort of slipway. But imagine, for the sake of the exercise, that you are at each end at sea level, but that in between you have to cross a central ridge which rises gradually from both coasts and that the only way to do it is by a series of locks. The heights of the epistle are reached in chapter 8, a sustained climax which takes the argument across the watershed. Up to that point we are going up the whole time, from that point we are going down. On the way up each of the locks, as it were, raises the water to a new level, introducing us to the stretch that follows. On the way down the locks represent the close or summary of the stretch of water in which we have been before the level drops again. We can represent it diagrammatically thus:

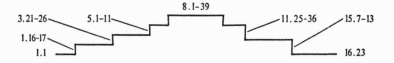

Introduction

We are now ready to embark on the journey. I shall take sections of the New English Bible text of varying lengths determined by the structure of the argument rather than by conveniently equal portions for Bible reading. I shall also, like a guide to an ancient building, proceed rapidly through some rooms and pause for a long time in others, rather than comment on everything we pass through. For the primary object is not to do justice to the details of the text for its own sake. It is to keep the company of one who described himself as 'a skilled master-builder' (I Cor. 3.10) and of those who have lived and loved and argued in the house since. We shall be enriched by the experience to the extent that we allow ourselves to stay our step at those points where most has been contended for and, to adapt the words of another mighty craftsman, 'not to stir without' giving to 'great argument' the attention it requires.

The Letter of Paul to the
ROMANS

The Gospel according to Paul

1 From Paul, servant of Christ Jesus, apostle by God's call, set apart for the service of the Gospel.

2 This gospel God announced beforehand in sacred scriptures
3 through his prophets. It is about his Son: on the human level he was born of David's stock, but on the level of the spirit – the
4 Holy Spirit – he was declared Son of God by a mighty act in that he rose from the dead:*a* it is about Jesus Christ our Lord.
5 Through him I received the privilege of a commission in his name to lead to faith and obedience men in all nations, yourselves
6 among them, you who have heard the call and belong to Jesus Christ.

7 I send greetings to all of you in Rome whom God loves and has called to be his dedicated people. Grace and peace to you from
, God our Father and the Lord Jesus Christ.

8 Let me begin by thanking my God, through Jesus Christ, for you all, because all over the world they are telling the story of
9 your faith. God is my witness, the God to whom I offer the humble service of my spirit by preaching the gospel of his Son:
10 God knows how continually I make mention of you in my prayers, and am always asking that by his will I may, somehow or
11 other, succeed at long last in coming to visit you. For I long to see
12 you; I want to bring you some spiritual gift to make you strong; or rather, I want to be among you to receive encouragement myself through the influence of your faith on me as of mine on you.

13 But I should like you to know,*b* my brothers, that I have often planned to come, though so far without success, in the hope of achieving something among you, as I have in other parts of the
14 world. I am under obligation to Greek and non-Greek, to
15 learned and simple: hence my eagerness to declare the Gospel to you in Rome as well as to others.

a. Or declared Son of God with full powers from the time when he rose from the dead.
b. Some witnesses read I believe you know.

This represents Paul's own Introduction and need not detain us long in view of the previous discussion of his plans and purpose.

Verses 3–4. This is widely held to be a pre-Pauline formula. Its balance is subsequently expanded by Matthew when he sets side by side the genealogy of Jesus, what he was 'at the human level', and his divine conception, what he was 'on the level of the spirit'. Both are to be held together, not one at the expense of the other – as happens when the virgin birth is made an *alternative* to his physical generation. At one level Jesus was genuinely the product of the processes of heredity and environment. Yet he is not to be accounted for exhaustively in terms of them: there is also a divine dimension and initiative.

There are interesting connections between this formula and the report of the Pauline preaching in Acts 13.17–41.

(a) Only here and in Acts 13.33 is Jesus proclaimed as 'Son' in any early preaching summary. Is this presentation peculiarly remembered as having been associated with Paul? Cf. Acts 9.20, where we read that Paul 'straightaway preached Jesus that this is the Son of God' (he is the only person who does so in Acts), and Gal. 1.16, 'he was pleased to reveal his Son in me'.

(b) The declaration of his sonship is associated with the resurrection. So too in Acts 13.33, quoting Ps. 2.7, 'this day have I begotten thee'.

(c) He is 'of David's stock' both here and in Acts 13.23.

The word 'declared' (*horisthentos*), used also in Acts 10.42; 17.31, means that he was at this point marked out (from other men) as Son of God. It does not imply that he then *became* the Son of God, as *genomenos* implies that he came into being at the human level, but that his unique Sonship then became clear to men. For he was already God's Son (Rom. 1.3; cf. 8.3,32). The logic is the same as in Phil. 2.6–10: he was in the form (or image) of God, and then at his resurrection received the titles of glory. For declared 'with power' (*en dynamei*), we may compare the contrast implied in Mark 9.1, of the kingdom of God still to come 'with power'.

The Holy Spirit here is literally 'the Spirit of holiness', which
14

is a Hebraism (cf., e.g., Ps. 51.11; Isa. 63.10–11). Paul retains it in order to preserve the contrast between 'in the sphere of flesh' and 'in the sphere of spirit', which is also to be found in I Peter 3.18; 4.6; I Tim. 3.16.

1.16–17

16   For I am not ashamed of the Gospel. It is the saving power of God for everyone who has faith – the Jew first, but the Greek
17   also – because here is revealed God's way of righting wrong, a way that starts from faith and ends in faith;^{a} as Scripture says, 'he shall gain life who is justified through faith'.

a Or ... wrong. It is based on faith and addressed to faith.

This is the first of the 'locks' of which I spoke, introducing the level that follows. It states the thesis that Paul is to expound in the first quarter of the epistle. The theme is only played over here as in an overture. We shall discuss its key words, 'righteousness' and 'faith', when they are taken up and expanded in 3.21–26.

It is not untypical, as we shall see, that Paul's first use of scripture should, by our standards, be a misuse. His interpretation of Hab. 2.4 requires 'by faith' to be linked with 'righteous' and not, as in the original, with 'shall live': it is the man who is 'righteous on the basis of faith' that will live. Paul also puts an interpretation on faith quite contrary to that which it has in Habakkuk, where the NEB correctly renders it 'the righteous man will live by being faithful'. For Habakkuk faith means faithfulness, as regularly in the Old Testament. Confronted by the Chaldean invasion the righteous man is to preserve his life by absolute loyalty to God through thick and thin. Here faith is very near to 'sheer character' (Dodd) – which is what Paul means by 'works'. Again, Paul's meaning is very different from

15

the use to which the Rabbis put the text, to mean righteousness by faithfulness to the law. The nearest approach to Paul is now to be found in the Dead Sea Scrolls Commentary on Habakkuk (1Qp. Hab. 8.1–3), which interprets Hab. 2.4 thus: 'Its meaning concerns all the doers of the Law in the house of Judah whom God will deliver from the house of judgment for the sake of their labour and their faith in the Teacher of Righteousness.' Here we get an interesting combination of 'justification' (deliverance from the house of judgment) and 'faith' as trust in a person. This is half way to Paul, but still fundamentally justification by works: it is the doers of the law who are to be justified for the sake of their labour – and by their faith in the Teacher of Righteousness, which probably means by their reliance on him as an interpreter of the Torah.

1.18–32

18 For we see divine retribution revealed from heaven and falling upon all the godless wickedness of men. In their wickedness they
19 are stifling the truth. For all that may be known of God by men lies plain before their eyes; indeed God himself has disclosed it
20 to them. His invisible attributes, that is to say his everlasting power and deity, have been visible, ever since the world began, to the eye of reason, in the things he has made. There is therefore
21 no possible defence for their conduct; knowing God, they have refused to honour him as God, or to render him thanks. Hence all their thinking has ended in futility, and their misguided minds
22 are plunged in darkness. They boast of their wisdom, but they
23 have made fools of themselves, exchanging the splendour of immortal God for an image shaped like mortal man, even for images like birds, beasts, and creeping things.
24 For this reason God has given them up to the vileness of their own desires, and the consequent degradation of their bodies,
25 because they have bartered away the true God for a false one,[a] and have offered reverence and worship to created things instead

16

of to the Creator, who is blessed for ever; amen.

26 In consequence, I say, God has given them up to shameful
27 passions. Their women have exchanged natural intercourse for
    unnatural, and their men in turn, giving up natural relations with
    women, burn with lust for one another; males behave indecently
    with males, and are paid in their own persons the fitting wage of
    such perversion.
28 Thus, because they have not seen fit to acknowledge God, he
    has given them up to their own depraved reason. This leads them
29 to break all rules of conduct. They are filled with every kind of
    injustice, mischief, rapacity, and malice; they are one mass of
30 envy, murder, rivalry, treachery, and malevolence; whisperers
    and scandal-mongers, hateful to God, insolent, arrogant, and
    boastful; they invent new kinds of mischief, they show no loyalty
31 to parents, no conscience, no fidelity to their plighted word; they
32 are without natural affection and without pity. They know well
    enough the just decree of God, that those who behave like this
    deserve to die, and yet they do it; not only so, they actually
    applaud such practices.

a Or the truth of God for the lie.

Having stated his theme, Paul launches into a long description
of the obverse of it – the state of man prior to faith and this new
righteousness of God. This is characterized not simply by the
absence of God, but by the 'wrath' of God – the positive
absence of God. Moreover, it is a state of affairs which is as
much a matter of revelation as its opposite: 'The righteousness
(*dikaiosynē*) of God is revealed' (1.17), 'the wrath (*orgē*) of
God is revealed' (1.18). In fact the full laying bare of the fearful
truth and final consequences of the alienation of human society
from God is but the other side of the very same revelation which
is God's way of righting wrong. It is only *as a Christian* that Paul
can understand the full measure of sin and the extent of God's
alienation from it – only in the revelation of the 'righteousness'
is the revelation of the 'wrath'. And yet conversely, as Barrett
points out, the 'for' at the beginning of verse 18 provides the
ground for the confidence that the longed-for vindication and
righteousness of God has indeed been revealed – for look

around you and you can see 'the wrath'. And this is essentially something which belongs to the last times: it is the eschatological reckoning, 'the wrath to come' (cf. 2.5; 5.9; etc.). But here it is in operation before the time. The last judgment is already 'on' – as in John 3.18–19, etc. It is being revealed; it is happening before your very eyes.

But what does the *orgē* mean?

Let us start from the fact to which Dodd draws attention in his commentary at this point, the fact of its impersonality. Paul never says that God is angry, as he says that God is loving and gracious. In fact only here and in Col. 3.6 = Eph. 5.6 is it specifically the wrath *of God* (though it is probably 'his' wrath in Rom. 9.22, but this is not explicit). Frequently he uses it in a curiously impersonal way – e.g., in 4.15; 'the law produces wrath' – of an objective condition, like 'death'. 'Wrath' is the process of inevitable retribution which comes into operation when God's laws are broken. It contains the idea of what happens in the life of a man or society when moral control is loosened. It is what takes over if the situation is allowed to rip. Cf. 1.24,26,28, 'God gave them over', he leaves pagan society to stew in its own juice. The retribution which overtakes it, resulting in automatic moral degradation, is what 'comes on' almost like a thermostat when, as it were, the moral temperature drops below a certain point. This is part of God's order and it works automatically: men need not and should not themselves attempt to 'adjust the set'. 'Beloved, never avenge yourselves, but leave it to the *orgē*' (12.19) – allow God's own workings to correct the balance. Compare 13.4, where the secular arm is seen as God's servant for retribution upon the offender – *ekdikos eis orgēn*: it is a mechanism by which the *orgē* is set in motion.

There is a certain impersonality about *orgē* which allows Dodd to say of the biblical writers that 'in speaking of wrath and judgement' they 'have their minds mainly on events, actual or expected, conceived as the inevitable results of sin; and when they speak of mercy they are thinking mainly of the personal relationship between God and his people'. Wrath is an *effectus* not an *affectus* (or emotion) – an effect of human sin, in a way that mercy is not an effect of human goodness. There is a lack of parallelism here, and an important truth in what Dodd stresses. Yet he has undoubtedly been shown to be one-sided (cf. D. E. Whiteley, *The Theology of St Paul*, 1964, pp. 61–72).

For the fact remains that a Jew never pictured God working by impersonal, automatic laws like a thermostat (which is my illustration not Dodd's). Wrath is essentially the perversion of a *personal* relationship. It is, whether expressed or unexpressed, the wrath *of God*, and in this key passage it is very clearly expressed: 'The wrath of God is revealed from heaven upon all the godless wickedness of men.' This need not, as Cranfield stresses, mean attributing to God capricious or irrational rage, but a deeply personal abhorrence, such as love must always feel in the presence of injustice or cruelty. Indeed, it is just this personal quality of it that saves the human situation. When God 'hands over' the sinner or human society he does not abandon it to anything outside himself. The condition of chaos and degeneration which Paul goes on to depict in the following verses is not simply a chaos and degeneration *against* the will of God, but a chaos and degeneration which *embodies* the will of God. What the wrath of God means is not indeed that God is furious with us. It does not express his emotion; but it does express his responsibility. It says that the mess we see around us is still God's mess, that, incredible as it may seem, it actually embodies, under the aspect of 'wrath', the *dikaiosynē* or righteous love of God. It expresses not merely an impersonal chaos, but a personal relationship. The *effectus* is under the control of an *affectus*, which is his love. The juice in which we are stewing is *his* juice, not simply our own. And this juice is not a specially concocted mixture of gall and brimstone alien to his nature and other than his love. It is not he who has gone sour on us, but we on him: being what we are, we are capable of knowing the wine of the divine love only as the vinegar of his wrath. *He* has not changed – the revelation of his righteousness and of his wrath are in fact one and the same revelation. Indeed, it is this inalienable personal quality of the wrath, even as wrath, the fact that

19

we cannot sin ourselves out of the structure of our being as persons in personal relationship with God, which is the *saving* factor in our otherwise desperate situation.

There is a resolute refusal throughout the Bible to allow that any person or thing or event can fall out of this personal relationship to God. Nothing can ever be merely impersonal in this universe: to say that it can is a denial of the existence of God. 'If disaster falls on a city, has not the Lord been at work?' (Amos 3.6). Substitute 'love' for 'the Lord' and you get the New Testament version of it. The New Testament insists on preserving the recognition that even the most iron laws of cause and effect, physical and moral, represent in the last analysis the operation of the divine love. And this fact the worst that evil may do cannot finally make void – because the worst evil is still itself the manifestation of the divine *orgē*. That is the ultimate guarantee that this world remains God's world and even the most distorted humanity God's humanity. The divine wrath is the saving guarantee that God has not and cannot let men go – beyond himself. The process of disintegration which moral retribution brings in its train is still the expression not of an iron *karma* but of a personal, and even of a loving, will. Once that principle of interpretation is abandoned, faith has no theology of secular history. In fact it is only because in chapter 1 Paul has surveyed and interpreted the whole of history in terms of God's wrath that he can go on in chapter 8 to survey and interpret it all *without exception* in terms of God's love.

It is not that in the interval God changes, or that he is vindictive to those that hate him and loving towards those that love him, or that he acts impersonally towards the one and personally towards the others. He is the same, it is his same 'righteousness' throughout, but all depends on whether a man is 'right' with him or not. It is man's condition of alienation or estrangement that forces the divine love to come *to him* as wrath. 'God's wrath is the "adverse wind" of the divine will which he comes to feel who runs into it' (Brunner). And since sin always depersonalizes, wrath is love coming to man as something impersonal. That is the truth which Dodd is concerned to bring out. If men will have it so, God's love must reach them through the channels that sin creates, meeting them as law rather than as love. What sin does is to transform man's inescapable personal relationship to God from a relationship which feels like being at home to a relationship which feels like being in prison. But from God's side it is the same relationship all the time – and what is more the very imprisonment, the wrath, is itself a *saving* necessity, and not merely retributive. So Paul looking back over the whole divine process is compelled to exclaim: 'In making all men *prisoners* to disobedience, God's purpose was to show mercy to all mankind. O depth of wealth, wisdom and knowledge in God!' (Rom. 11.32–33).

But this is to anticipate. Paul has first to 'include all men under disobedience' – to show that before *any* can be saved *all* are lost. So in chapters 1 and 2 he sets out to demonstrate the complete universality of sin and wrath and of man's alienation from any saving relationship with God, first in relation to the Gentile world and then in relation even to the Jews, the very instrument of God's saving mission.

The first charge against the Gentile world is that they deliberately or unconsciously *suppress* the truth. There is a striking parallel here, as in much of Paul's argument in Romans, with II Esdras, a Jewish apocalypse written about AD 100: 'God has given clear instructions for all men when they come into this world, telling them how to attain life and how to escape punishment. But the ungodly have refused to obey him; they have set up their own empty ideas, and planned deceit and wickedness; they have even denied the existence of the Most High and have not acknowledged his ways' (7.21–24). It is not merely, as the Greek philosophers had said, that sin is ignorance – or if there is ignorance it is culpable ignorance. They are without excuse or defence. Why? Because whatever men can know of God they have *en autois*, within them or among them. For God has disclosed it to them. 'His invisible attributes, that is to say his everlasting power and deity, have been visible, ever since the world began, to the eye of reason, in the things he has made' (verses 19–20).

21

Paul's language is here influenced by the language of popular Stoicism, the scientific humanism of his day, which had already been combined with Jewish thought, particularly in a book like that of Wisdom which, as will become clear, appears to have influenced Paul extensively. We may compare Wisd. 13.1–9, where there is the same argument leading to the same conclusion that men are 'without excuse' for not recognizing the Creator in the creature. Both 'invisible' as a divine attribute is found in Wisd. 2.23 and *theiotēs*, divinity, for the first and only time in the biblical literature in Wisd. 18.9. Compare *to theion*, the Deity, in Acts 17.30, when Paul is addressing such a Stoic audience. Both passages (Rom. 1 and Acts 17) are in fundamental unanimity and a good commentary on the presuppositions Paul was prepared to allow when commending the gospel to such an audience. Quite clearly there is a 'point of contact' with God outside Christ – he is not far from any one of us, we are his offspring (Acts 17.27–28). Paul thus specifically contradicts the Barthian denial of any point of contact, any revelation, outside Christ. Brunner convicted Barth here of being unbiblical: mankind has no excuse precisely because there *is* a general revelation through creation.

Equally Paul contradicts the Thomist view that man can by his own reason know God, apart from revelation. Man does not know some things by reason and some by revelation – but all by revelation. Even the pagan world can know only 'because God himself has disclosed it to them' (verse 19).

But while Paul fully allows for a natural revelation he provides little confidence for a natural theology. Here St Thomas Aquinas is, I believe, clearly unbiblical. He assumes that man's reason working on the natural revelation can build up a coherent and, as far as it goes, entirely correct view of the nature and attributes of God. The whole of his *Summa Theologica* I, up to the doctrine of the Trinity (which like the Incarnation is perceived only by revelation), is grounded on natural reason alone, and this foundation is never subsequently modified or corrected in the light of biblical insights. It need not be, because natural reason is a perfectly adequate instrument as far as it goes.

But this is precisely what Paul proceeds to deny. It ought to be adequate, but in fact it isn't. 'Their thinking has ended in futility, and their misguided minds are plunged in darkness' (verse 21). And the reason is that 'knowing God, they have refused to honour him as God, or to render him thanks'. In other words, knowledge of God is not just something intellectual: it is an acknowledgment of God *as God*, a recognition which is given only in the true worship of God, in the unconditional worth accorded him as the centre of the whole of life. That is why (verses 22–23) false worship, idolatry, is at the very heart of the intellectual error – for idolatry is simply confusing the image of God (mental as well as metal) with God. Where this relationship is distorted, where the centre of men's lives is not God but themselves, then reason becomes rationalization, and natural theology in some degree or other a reflection simply of man's ideas of God – ideas which are in some measure degraded, depersonalized, or merely add up to the still-life deity of the philosophers who makes no claims.

All this is summed up in verse 28: 'Because they have not seen fit (*ouk edokimasan*) to acknowledge God, he has given them up to their own depraved reason (*adokimon noun*).' The *nous*, a term taken over by Paul from Greek thinking, is the faculty by which men should come to the knowledge and acknowledgment of God (cf. 7.28). Its function is *dokimazein*, to make moral and spiritual judgments (cf. 2.18). But moral obliquity renders it *adokimos*, incapable of such discernment or discrimination. This is only another way of saying that reason is 'fallen': like all the rest of man's being it is off-centre, 'turned in upon itself' (Luther). In purely objective judgments, as in mathematics and the natural sciences, this distortion or 'curvature' of the human reason may be negligible. But whenever man's own place and status is affected, wherever existential judgments are involved which bring into question a person's own relationship towards what he is knowing, and pre-eminently in the knowledge of God, where man's whole position as the centre of his world is challenged quite radically, the distortion which comes from self-centredness and self-interest will become apparent. Where man's own standing is touched, reason quickly becomes rationalization. As in Marx, there is a direct connection between alienation and ideology. There is no such thing as a natural rightousness even in theology: reason as much as anything else requires to be justified by faith before it can function truly as reason. (On this see Brunner's *Revelation and Reason*, 1947, and Alan Richardson's *Christian Apologetics*, 1947, chapter 10).

But the *adokimos nous* involves and includes much more than crooked thinking. God gives them over to a depraved reason to 'break all the rules of conduct' (verse 28). Note the phrase 'God gave them over', which Paul repeats three times. As a form of judgment we may compare Ps. 106.15: 'He gave them what they asked but sent a wasting sickness among them'. The enjoyment of the chosen way is itself the punishment. Cf. Wisd. 11.16, 'To teach them that the instruments of a man's sin are the instruments of his punishment', or Rev. 22.11: 'Let the wicked man go on being still more wicked, let the filthy man be still more filthy' – let him wallow in it. If that is the cup a man chooses to drink, then he shall drink it to the dregs. So here God allows Gentile society to rip. He lets them taste the fruit of their own lusts: they are 'paid in their own persons the fitting wage of such perversion' (verse 27).

The sequence of thought (and many of the phrases) in Wisd. 13–14 is strikingly parallel: (1) natural religion discarded; (2) idolatry; leading to (3) a catalogue of immorality. Paul here summarizes the argument without actually quoting. His lists in verses 26–27 and 29–31 are in line with typical Stoic lists of vices (sensual and anti-social) and the second is introduced by the Stoic phrase 'that which is not fitting', i.e., not in line with the natural law on which society rests, and therefore wrong.

Paul has now analysed and condemned Gentile society, using its own terms and presuppositions, but bringing to bear upon them insights derived from the distinctively biblical dimension of the personal relationship to God. It is a model of theological method, corresponding to the method of 'correlation' or 'answering theology' of Paul Tillich. Now he turns to apply the same to the Jews.

2.1–16

2 You therefore have no defence – you who sit in judgement, whoever you may be – for in judging your fellow-man you con-
2 demn yourself, since you, the judge, are equally guilty. It is admitted that God's judgement is rightly passed upon all who
3 commit such crimes as these; and do you imagine – you who pass judgement on the guilty while committing the same crimes your-self – do you imagine that you, any more than they, will escape
4 the judgement of God? Or do you think lightly of his wealth of kindness, of tolerance, and of patience, without recognizing that
5 God's kindness is meant to lead you to a change of heart? In the rigid obstinacy of your heart you are laying up for yourself a
6 store of retribution for the day of retribution, when God's just judgement will be revealed, and he will pay every man for what
7 he has done. To those who pursue glory, honour, and immortal-ity by steady persistence in well-doing, he will give eternal life;
8 but for those who are governed by selfish ambition, who refuse obedience to the truth and take the wrong for their guide, there
9 will be the fury of retribution. There will be grinding misery for every human being who is an evil-doer, for the Jew first and for
10 the Greek also; and for every well-doer there will be glory, hon-our, and peace, for the Jew first and also for the Greek.
11 12 For God has no favourites: those who have sinned outside the pale of the Law of Moses will perish outside its pale, and all who
13 have sinned under that law will be judged by the law. It is not by hearing the law, but by doing it, that men will be justified before
14 God. When Gentiles who do not possess the law carry out its precepts by the light of nature, then, although they have no law,
15 they are their own law, for they display the effect of the law inscribed on their hearts. Their conscience is called as witness, and their own thoughts argue the case on either side, against
16 them or even for them, on the day when God judges the secrets of human hearts through Christ Jesus. So my gospel declares.

The final charge of chapter 1 is that those he is condemning not only do these things – they actually applaud such practices, they even regard them as right and proper (verse 32). He now (2.1) turns to those who do not applaud, in fact they condemn heartily – but they still practise what they condemn. Primarily no doubt he has the Jew here in mind, but it is not in fact until verse 17 that he turns specifically to the Jews. Verses 9–16 clearly envisage both Jew and Greek, and the introduction 'You, whoever you are, who sit in judgement' is deliberately vague, to include all who take their stand on a high moral code whether Jew or pagan moralist. What joins them both with those whom they condemn is the term 'without excuse or defence' (2.1; cf. 1.20).

In verse 4 the Jew presumes upon the goodness and forebearance of God, which he complacently interprets as a sure sign of his favour towards the chosen people. There is again an interesting parallel with the book of Wisdom. Cf. Wisd. 12.22: 'So we are chastened by thee, but our enemies thou dost scourge ten thousand times more, so that we may lay thy goodness to heart when we sit in judgement.' And then, after describing in chapters 13 and 14 the rake's progress of the pagan world through natural religion, idolatry and immorality, the author goes on in 15.1–5: 'But thou, our God, art kind and true and patient, a merciful ruler of all that is. For even if we sin, we are thine; we acknowledge thy power. But we will not sin, because we know that we are accounted thine. . . . *We* have not been led astray by the perverted inventions of human skill or the barren labours of painters, by some gaudy painted shape, the sight of which arouses in fools a passionate desire for a mere image without life or breath.' This is incidentally an insight into the smug philistinism of contemporary Judaism in the matter of the representational arts. For similar Jewish complacency *vis-à-vis* pagans, cf. II Esdras 3.28–36: 'Weigh our sins in the balance against the sins of the rest of the world; and it will be clear which way the scale tips. . . . Has any nation ever kept your commandments like Israel? You may find one man here, one there; but nowhere a whole nation.'

God's kindness is meant, of course, to lead not to complacency but to a change of heart, as again in Wisd. 11.23: 'But thou art merciful to all men ...; thou dost overlook the sins of men to bring them to repentance.' To this question of the forbearance of God in overlooking sin and suspending punishment Paul returns in 3.26 and 9.22. But meanwhile he reminds his readers in verse 6 that 'he will pay every man for what he has done'. This is in full accord with the consistent Pauline, and New Testament, position that while men are justified by faith they are judged by works.

Observe in verses 11–12 that the lack of favouritism in God does not mean that all men are in exactly the same position, nor does it deny election and privilege. It is that reward and punishment are without any partiality taking into account differences with which each start. It is the same principle enunciated in Amos 3.2: 'For you alone have I cared among all the nations of the world; therefore will I punish you for all your iniquities.'

Observe too that verse 13, 'it is not by hearing the law, but by doing it, that men will be justified before God', comes from Paul and not from James! By the law it is *deeds* which are required for acquittal. Paul's later charge is precisely that no one can in fact show these deeds, the law cannot produce the works, and therefore always issues in a verdict of 'guilty'.

In verses 14–15 Paul again shows as in chapter 1 how far he is prepared to go in taking over the ideas of contemporary scientific humanism. His sentiments are almost pure Stoicism. For the law of nature apprehended by the immanent reason in every man there are many parallels quoted by the commentators. We may note especially Plutarch: 'Law ... which is not written on papyrus rolls or wooden tablets, but is his own reason within the soul, which perpetually dwells with him and guards him and never leaves the soul bereft of leadership', and Aristotle: 'The cultivated and free-minded man will so behave as being a law unto himself' (Notice the change in meaning of this phrase – it now means recognizing no law!). Already this way of thinking had been fused with Judaism in Philo of Alexandria, who speaks of the Patriarchs (who since they lived before Moses could not know the law in its written form) as themselves 'laws endowed with life and reason'. Especially Stoic are the phrases *physei*, 'by nature', and *syneidēsis*, 'conscience', which first occurs in biblical Greek in this sense again in Wisd. 17.10. Conscience for the Stoics and for Paul is not the *source* of moral obligation (as in our phrase, 'my conscience tells me I must do this') – that is the law of nature; nor is it used of the individual standing out against society or authority (as in 'the nonconformist conscience'). It is that which in every man acknowledges the law as binding – the sense of 'ought', or more often of guilt when one fails. Conscience is *common* moral knowledge (*syn*eidēsis, *con*scientia), appealing, in the words of the Ministry of Transport's advertisements, to the presupposition, 'You know it ˙makes sense'. When this presupposition is absent – as it was for so many in the Papal encyclical on contraception – natural law loses its authority.

Paul proceeds to justify his 'liberal' view that the Gentiles even though outside the law of Moses nevertheless do have a law in their lives. For this he adduces three pieces of evidence: (1) the sheer fruits of their conduct – there are good men outside the church; (2) the added testimony of the fact of conscience – their goodness is not just a matter of accident or temperament: they acknowledge a real sense of obligation; (3) the signs of genuine moral conflict, which there would not be if they really believed in no objective moral law, if all ethical judgments could be reduced to the level of 'I like mustard, I don't' – for there is no arguing about tastes. Notice that 'their own thoughts argue the case on either side, against them or *even* for them' – accusing, or it may be actually excusing, them. Paul is a commonsense realist with no doctrinaire prejudgments in this matter of non-Christian morality. He allows for 'nature' being a good thing, for real moral distinctions and real moral attainments, and doesn't try to make out that pagan virtues are only splendid vices. On the other hand he knows that it is men's bad conscience even more than their good which is the most telling witness to the law of God, and that ultimately nature, like religion, is powerless to give a right relationship to God. If going to church ('circumcision') doesn't of itself bring a man to God, then merely living a decent life and never doing anyone any harm doesn't either.

Finally, in verse 16, both Jewish and pagan doctrine is subsumed under the only specifically Christian statement in the chapter – a note of judgment. What distinguishes 'my', i.e., the Christian gospel, is 'through Christ Jesus'. Hence its emphatic position in the Greek at the end of the sentence. It is noticeable how this insistence on judgment through Jesus is also the only specifically Christian statement in Paul's sermon at Athens (Acts 17.31) – at any rate as far as he was allowed to finish it.

2.17–29

---

17 But as for you – you may bear the name of Jew; you rely upon
18 the law and are proud of your God; you know his will; you are
     aware of moral distinctions because you receive instruction from
19 the law; you are confident that you are the one to guide the blind,
20 to enlighten the benighted, to train the stupid, and to teach the
     immature, because in the law you see the very shape of knowl-
21 edge and truth. You, then, who teach your fellow-man, do you
     fail to teach yourself? You proclaim, 'Do not steal'; but are you
22 yourself a thief? You say, 'Do not commit adultery'; but are you
     an adulterer? You abominate false gods; but do you rob their
23 shrines? While you take pride in the law, you dishonour God by
24 breaking it. For, as Scripture says, 'Because of you the name of
     God is dishonoured among the Gentiles.'
25 Circumcision has value, provided you keep the law; but if you
     break the law, then your circumcision is as if it had never been.
26 Equally, if an uncircumcised man keeps the precepts of the law,
27 will he not count as circumcised? He may be uncircumcised in his
     natural state, but by fulfilling the law he will pass judgement on
     you who break it, for all your written code and your circumci-
28 sion. The true Jew is not he who is such in externals, neither is
29 the true circumcision the external mark in the flesh. The true Jew

29

is he who is such inwardly, and the true circumcision is of the heart, directed not by written precepts but by the Spirit; such a man receives his commendation not from men but from God.

Paul now turns to his real charge against the Jew, whom he mentions specifically by name for the first time – his failure to produce conduct in line with his great privileges.

The phrase in verse 18 *dokimazein ta diapheronta* means either to make moral distinctions – in contrast with the *adokimos nous* of the Gentiles; or to approve, after testing, the things that are more excellent. Probably in the context it means the former.

In verse 19, the words 'you are confident that you are the one to ...' or 'you fancy yourself as' are especially pointed with reference to Jews abroad, and perhaps particularly ironical in Rome, where 'it is difficult to say which is more conspicuous, the repulsion or the attraction which the Jews exercised upon the heathen world' (Sanday and Headlam). For their unsavoury reputation we have Juvenal's blistering satire, 14.96ff. The same claim to be the guides of the blind doubtless lies behind Jesus's remark in Matt. 15.4 (cf. 23.16, 24). Yet there is no compelling evidence that Paul has Jesus's saying specifically in mind.

In verses 21–24, Barrett argues that this does not mean that the typical Jew was really as crudely immoral as his pagan neighbour: 'it is simply not true that the average Jewish missionary acted in this way'. He thinks Paul is doing what Jesus does in Matt. 5.21–48 – taking the commandments and saying that in their inwardness every Jew is breaking them: as a nation, in its relation to God, Israel is committing robbery (Mal. 3.8–9), adultery (Hos. 1–3; Jer. 38), and sacrilege by its failure to give glory to God alone. This certainly gives good sense – though verse 24 ('because of you the name of God is blasphemed among the Gentiles') does suggest that it is what pagan outsiders can see and not only what God can see that causes the scandal. It is better probably to stick to the literal sense. Jews were not above robbing pagan shrines, which were regarded as fair game – indeed it was meritorius to tear down idols. (Cf. Acts 19.37, where Paul is said by the town-clerk of Ephesus *not* to be a temple-robber, as might perhaps have been expected from a Jew.) The quotation in verse 24 is characteristic of Paul's use of scripture – he takes the words but turns the meaning to his own use. In Isa. 52.5 (following the Greek text) 'it was owing to the misery and helplessness of the people of God, in exile among the nations, that the heathen scoffed at the divine name' (Dodd): 'The God of Israel is not able to deliver his people: he is no God.' Now God is scoffed because of the inconsistency between the high Jewish pretensions and *their* low behaviour.

In verse 29, 'in spirit, not in letter' does not mean, as it does for us, 'in true intention' as opposed to 'in outward observance only', but 'directed not by written precepts but by the Spirit'. It is the same contrast as in Matt. 3.11 between baptism 'in water' and 'in spirit'. The latter does not refer to being 'baptised in spirit' (i.e., truly and inwardly), but 'by the Spirit'. *Gramma* is a written document or code. It is part of Paul's charge against the law that not only is it given as double remove from God, 'by angels and through an intermediary (Moses)' (Gal. 3.19), but that it is a 'dispensation of letter and not spirit' (II Cor. 3.6–7, the critical passage for its interpretation). The letter 'kills' because it merely sets down in cold print what you must do: it does not give you the power to keep its commandments. As in John 6.63, it is only spirit which gives life. Similarly in Rom. 7.6, the newness of spirit and the oldness of the letter, refers to the difference between the two dispensations – not to the spirit and letter *of the law*.

In verse 29 commentators allude to the play on the name Jew, *Judaios*. Judah means 'praise' (Gen. 29.35; 49.8). Barrett seeks to get it by a punning translation: 'he is a Jew, whose due comes not from men but from God'.

3 Then what advantage has the Jew? What is the value of circumci-
2 sion? Great, in every way. In the first place, the Jews were
3 entrusted with the oracles of God. What if some of them were
unfaithful? Will their faithlessness cancel the faithfulness of
4 God? Certainly not! God must be true though every man living
were a liar; for we read in Scripture, 'When thou speakest thou
shalt be vindicated, and win the verdict when thou art on trial.'

5 Another question: if our injustice serves to bring out God's
justice, what are we to say? Is it unjust of God (I speak of him in
6 human terms) to bring retribution upon us? Certainly not! If
God were unjust, how could he judge the world?

7 Again, if the truth of God brings him all the greater honour
because of my falsehood, why should I any longer be condemned
8 as a sinner? Why not indeed 'do evil that good may come', as
some libellously report me as saying? To condemn such men as
these is surely no injustice.

9 What then? Are we Jews any better off?[a] No, not at all![b] For
we have already formulated the charge that Jews and Greeks
10 alike are all under the power of sin. This has scriptural warrant:

'There is no just man, not one;
11 no one who understands, no one who seeks God.
12 All have swerved aside, all alike have become debased;
There is no one to show kindness; no, not one.

13 Their throat is an open grave,
they use their tongues for treachery,
adders' venom is on their lips,
14 and their mouth is full of bitter curses.

15 Their feet hasten to shed blood,
16 ruin and misery lie along their paths,
17 they are strangers to the high-road of peace,
18 and reverence for God does not enter their thoughts.'

19 Now all the words of the law are addressed, as we know, to
those who are within the pale of the law, so that no one may have
anything to say in self-defence, but the whole world may be
20 exposed to the judgement of God. For (again from Scripture) 'no

32

human being can be justified in the sight of God' for having kept
the law: law brings only the consciousness of sin.

a *Or* Are we Jews any worse off?
b *Or* Not in all respects.

In the first eight verses of this chapter we have three objections
from imaginary opponents, no doubt reflecting Paul's actual
experience in disputation with Jews, but objections also arising
in his own mind as a Jew.

Verses 1–2. Has not the previous argument proved too
much? Is there any distinction left between Jew and Gentile?
Answer: Yes, the promises.

Verses 3–4. Has not Jewish unbelief cancelled these promises? Answer: No. Unfaithfulness cannot make God unfaithful;
in fact it simply acts as a foil to God's faithfulness.

Verses 5–8. But if this is the case, why should God condemn
men for doing him such a good service? That needs no answer:
it is plainly casuistical.

Notice, in verse 3, 'some of them were unfaithful'. Paul's
conclusion in verses 9–20 is that *all* the Jews as well as *all* the
pagan world are under sin. But he allows here again for *relative*
moral distinctions, as he did in the case of the Gentiles (2.14–
15). Moreover he has in mind that there *was* a faithful remnant.
This he will elaborate in chapters 9–11. See Dodd's excellent
note on this passage in the light of the later and fuller argument.

Verses 6 and 8 are typical of Paul's argument in these sort of
cases – especially again in 9.19–20 (How can the pot presume to
answer the potter back?). He doesn't resort to logic, but like the
book of Job is content to point to the 'infinite qualitative difference' (Kierkegaard) between God and man. The mere suggestion that human standards of judgment can be applied to God is
anthropomorphism. But such doubts nevertheless arise.

The fact is that in all these cases the objector is *logically* on
excellent ground. If sin is a '*felix culpa*' because it serves to show
more clearly the depths of the divine mercy and faithfulness,
then to go on sinning that 'there may be all the more grace'

33

(6.1) or 'to do evil that good may come' (3.8) *is* the logical consequence; and for God to punish what has been the direct means to his greater glory is ungracious to say the least. From the point of view of logic, from the standpoint of the spectator, that *is* the conclusion: *'pecca fortiter'*, sin boldly. But from the point of view of someone who really loves God and stands face to face with him in moral responsibility such a conclusion is unthinkable. If you know a person loves you and will go on loving you however unworthy you are, then logically you might say, 'Well, it doesn't matter now how badly I treat him or her – let's make the most of this blank cheque of love'. But in fact to someone actually within a real love-relationship, knowing it not from the touch-line, but from the inside, existentially, face to face with the other person's devotion, then the constraint is to do precisely the opposite. We may compare again the passage quoted earlier from Wisd. 15.1–2: 'But thou, O God, art kind and true and patient, a merciful ruler of all that is. For even if we sin we are thine.... But we will not sin, because we know that we are accounted thine.' There speaks the logic not of the spectator but of the I-Thou relation. And it is precisely this fact to which unerringly Paul goes back each time. Logically he puts up a pretty poor case, and he does not answer what are perfectly rational objections: he simply shuts the objector up. But he recognizes that in the last analysis these objections occur only if we put ourselves in an inauthentic relation to the whole matter. For they are questions that simply do not arise as long as we are standing in the genuine relationship of faith or love. And isn't it perfectly true from experience that *in* this relationship, whether of prayer or action, we are *not* in fact worried by the tension and logical incompatability between God's control of our lives and human freedom, between God's sovereignty over history and human responsibility for sin, between the fact that our sin has merited such a marvellous redemption and the knowledge that it is heinous without extenuation? These antinomies arise only when we stand back from the subject-subject relationship and theologize and argue about them in a subject-object relationship. (For a profound theological exploration of this difference, cf. Brunner, *Truth as Encounter*, 1964.) Paul with scant respect flings us back to the place where these objections wither in silence: 'such arguments are rightly condemned'.

After the interruption of these tiresome but nagging objections Paul resumes his argument in verse 9 with some words that have left the translators at sixes and sevens: *ti oun? proechometha? ou pantōs*. The NEB text renders them: 'Are we Jews any better off? No, not at all'. But it has two marginal readings: 'Are we Jews any worse off?' and 'Not in all respects'. These may be combined to mean almost anything! The arguments can be followed in the commentaries. I won't go into detail except to say that both Dodd and Barrett concur with the NEB (and RSV) text as the correct interpretation. Yet this is not even represented in the RV, which offers yet another translation in its margin: 'Do we excuse ourselves?'! But if the NEB text is right, why does Paul apparently give a contrary answer to that in 3.1: 'What advantage has the Jew? ... Great, in every way'?

But there is no real contradiction. The Jews have many advantages, yet ultimately they are in no better case. This is consistent with Paul's admission that there *are* relative moral distinctions and privileges and yet *vis-à-vis* God, in reference to the vital question of salvation, of being right with him, all are in exactly the same position. He concedes that Gentiles do by nature the things of the law (2.14–15) – yet they are all of them hopelessly under sin (3.9). He concedes that Jews have real assets and that some of them were more unfaithful than others (3.1–3): yet, in relation to God, for the purposes of standing before him, they are in exactly the same hopeless case as the Gentiles (3.9). The Jews have advantages – bags of them – yet for all that they are not a scrap better off. In other words, *to perisson* in 3.1 means the initial advantage, the odds on, *proechometha* in 3.9 refers to the state of the race, the lie of the field. The Jew is given a tremendous handicap, yet he doesn't win. But neither does the Gentile; for both alike fail to finish.

The difference is that whereas Paul can put the Gentiles out of the running with a single knock-out blow (chapter 1), he has to keep on coming back at the Jew, who thinks he can parry each thrust in turn. So this is where Paul keeps on bearing down right through chapter 2 and the first half of chapter 3. The Jew appeals to the law – but this does not shield him (2.1–24); he appeals to circumcision, but there is no refuge here either (2.25–29); he tries some casuistry – but that is brushed aside (3.1–8). So Paul comes to his conclusion: 'What then? Are we Jews any better off? No, not at all! For we have already formulated the charge, that Jews and Greeks alike are all under the power of sin.' And finally, should the Jew try to wriggle out of this bracketing with the Gentile, Paul turns to Israel's own scriptures; and largely from memory and without troubling over much about their context draws out of the armoury six texts to hurl at him. The Jew may still retort, 'Oh, but these texts refer to the Gentiles'. 'No,' says Paul (verse 19), 'the things in the law – or, as we should say, in the Bible – are spoken to those who are within the pale of the law', i.e., to Jews. This is a summary of Nygren's excellent exposition, and he concludes: 'It is manifest enough that the Gentiles who have not the law are sinners and under the wrath of God. When, therefore, the law stops the mouth of those who have the law, compelling them to confess that they are the veriest sinners, the result is clear. "The whole world lies exposed to the judgement of God".'

In verses 10–18 we have a catena of quotations (more or less free) from Ps. 14.1–3 (verses 10–12), Ps. 5.9 (verse 13a), Ps. 140.3 (verse 13b), Ps. 10.7 (verse 14), Isa. 59.7–8 (verses 15–17), Ps. 36.1 (verse 18) – all described as 'the law'. This catena has had an extraordinary history, affecting the text of the Greek translation of the Old Testament (the Septuagint or the LXX). The whole got read back *en bloc* into the text of Ps. 14 (LXX 13), carrying straight on from verse 3. The additional verses were included in the Textus Receptus and from there, through the Old Latin, got into the Vulgate, and thence the Great Bible and the Book of Common Prayer. Jerome put an obelus against the verses in his second edition, but it dropped out; Coverdale put an asterisk in his revision of the Great Bible, but it was ignored by the Prayer Book; finally in 1928 the Prayer Book revisers put them in brackets – but they have suffered much the same fate on the assumption that these brackets are there for the same reason as the others which they introduced into the psalter and that we now haven't such a weak stomach for cursing as those liberals back in the twenties! It's a lost cause to get anything out of scripture once it's in.

Finally, in verse 20, in support of his dogmatic (almost axiomatic) statement that no one can be justified in the sight of God for having kept the law, Paul is simply content to throw out the epigrammatic comment: 'Law brings only the consciousness of sin.' The effect of the law is merely to bring sin to consciousness: it cannot do anything else. It is the first of a series of unargued statements on the subject of the law which Paul throws out and which he does not take up or justify till chapter 7.

Meanwhile, having now established creation's universal need for the gospel and hopeless condition without it, he returns to elaborate the great theme he outlined originally in 1.17.

3.21–26

---

21 But now, quite independently of law, God's justice has been
22 brought to light. The Law and the prophets both bear witness to it: it is God's way of righting wrong, effective through faith in
23 Christ for all who have such faith – all, without distinction. For all alike have sinned, and are deprived of the divine splendour,
24 and all are justified by God's free grace alone, through his act of
25 liberation in the person of Christ Jesus. For God designed him to be the means of expiating sin by his sacrificial death, effective through faith. God meant by this to demonstrate his justice, because in his forbearance he had overlooked the sins of the past
26 – to demonstrate his justice now in the present, showing that he is both himself just and justifies any man who puts his faith in Jesus.

For a good discussion of this very dense passage see the commentaries of Dodd and Cranfield both here and on 1.17. First an analysis of the important words.

The righteousness of God (*dikaiosynē theou*). This is a term above all that cannot be understood except against the background of the Old Testament and especially of II Isaiah, for which Norman Snaith's *Distinctive Ideas of the Old Testament* (1944) provides a useful introduction. 'Righteousness' begins as an attribute of God – or better as an activity or act of God. For the Old Testament the attributes of God don't designate God as he is in himself but the relationship of God to his people, which is not something static and ready-made but something which God is constantly creating, bringing into reality, embodying in history. The divine attributes are not fully real till they have been realized, in events. So II Isaiah speaks of God's attributes 'going forth', hiving off from him and taking up their abode in his people, till there is something of God on both sides of the relationship. We may compare the Christian doctrine of the Holy Spirit: 'every virtue we possess is his alone'. This is especially true of God's righteousness and salvation, which are both attributes of God and conditions or characteristics of his people. Cf. Isa. 46.13: 'I will bring near my righteousness; it shall not be far off, and my salvation shall not tarry'; 51.5: 'my righteousness is near; my salvation is gone forth'. The final condition is when the circle is closed, when as it were God's attributes come back to him in the restoration of everything *in God*. Cf. C. Wesley: 'Till we see thy great salvation, perfectly restored in thee' (taking restored to apply to salvation not to us, as Wesley doubtless did not intend).

So too in Paul 'the righteousness of God is revealed'. It is both a righteousness which characterizes his life and the righteousness brought to us from him, a status of righteousness which is ours *before* him. It describes both sides of the relationship; and in neither case is it *primarily* an ethical category designating conduct, but a religious one characterizing a covenant-relationship of God with his people, both on his side and on the side of those who must stand in it towards him.

Of it we may make three points:

(a) It has no suggestion of justice *as opposed* to love. So far from being contrasted with God's saving activity, it is identified with it. Cf. Jer. 23.5–6; Ps. 31.1 ('deliver me in thy righteousness'); Isa. 45.21 ('a just God and a saviour'). We find the same thing now in the Dead Sea Manual of Discipline: 'In his compassion he has brought me near; and in his dependable mercy he will bring my justification. In his steadfast righteousness he has justified me and in his great goodness he will pardon (or, atone for) all my iniquities' (1 QS 11.13–14; cf. also 11.2–3 and 12). Of God's righteousness, Vincent Taylor writes: 'Within it there is a warmth which impels him towards salvation ... Love is implicit in righteousness, righteousness explicit in love' (*The Atonement in New Testament Teaching*, 1940, p. 112). Similarly Karl Barth: 'Righteousness in the Old Testament sense is not the righteousness of the judge who makes the debtor pay, but the action of a judge who in the accused recognizes the wretch whom he wishes to help by putting him to rights. That is what righteousness means. Righteousness means setting right. And that is what God does' (*Dogmatics in Outline*, 1949, p. 119). Or as L. Köhler puts it, 'In Hebrew, "to judge" and "to help" are parallel ideas. "Judge the fatherless", says the prophet (Isa. 1.17). This does not mean "condemn him", but "help him to his rights" ' (*Hebrew Man*, 1956, p. 157). And this is what Paul is referring to in 1.17 and 3.21 – so that in 3.24 God's righteousness is an expression of his grace or graciousness. It is a justice but a creative justice, 'a way of righting wrong'.

(b) In face of sin, righteousness refers to faithfulness to the demands of the relationship when this is impugned. It is used of the vindication of God (cf. Isa. 45.23). God proves himself always absolutely faithful or righteous (so Rom. 3.4–6; 9.14–15). He vindicates his *holy* love in the cross of Christ (3.26).

(c) It refers to the corresponding right standing or faithfulness to the demands of the covenant-relationship from the other side. It is the status or position of one who can stand before God in this relationship, who can face God upon his own terms. Such a man is righteous (*dikaios*) before God. Of course, in order to stand before the holy God on his terms, certain moral conditions are implicit. Yet 'righteousness' does not primarily designate the ethical standard but the religious standing, the status of being right with God. It is not so much goodness as God-acceptedness.

The verb 'to justify' (*dikaioō*) means to judge a man capable of this. It does not mean to make morally righteous. It means to pronounce acceptable, to declare that God accepts the person concerned as a son, as one who can stand in the covenant-relationship. This is exactly the process in the parable of the prodigal son – the father by putting a robe on him does not make or declare him morally innocent (like the pall of snow that is supposed to have fallen on the coffin of Charles I). There is no pretence. He does however declare, not simply in word but in deed, that he is accepting him as his son. The son is therefore justified, enabled to sit at his table with the status of a member of the family.

Barrett is right to stress that the insistence in the Reformed tradition that *dikaioō* does not mean to 'make righteous' but to 'count righteous' can lead to a disastrous weakening of the word to suggest a mere 'imputed' righteousness, a legal fiction. He insists that it really does mean to make righteous – for God achieves what he declares – so long as we remember that 'righteous' does not mean virtuous but right with God, clear, acquitted. 'Justification then means no legal fiction but an act of forgiveness on God's part, described in terms of the proceedings of a law court. Far from being a legal fiction, this is a creative act in the field of divine-human relations.'

It is of course part of the through-and-through ethical conception of God in Judaism that such justification must be intimately bound up with morality. It was fundamental that God could not justify, vindicate, acquit (for the word is a metaphor from the law-courts) the ungodly or sinners. Thus in Exod. 23.7 he is represented as saying: 'I will not justify the wicked.' Indeed it is a frequent charge against unjust judges in the Old Testament that they do precisely this: 'He that justifies the wicked, and he that condemns the righteous, both of them alike are an abomination to the Lord' (Prov. 17.15; cf. 24.24; Isa. 5.23). And we find exactly the same thing in the so-called Damascus Document of the Qumran community. Of the wicked it is said: 'They justified the wicked and condemned the righteous' (1.14), in contrast to God: 'who justified the righteous and condemned the wicked' (6.4). That contrast was axiomatic, even for a community which had such a sense of the saving initiative of God's righteousness: his justification must have respect to ethical realities. And this conviction is expressed by saying that a man is justified by observing the law. For it is thus that a man fulfils the demands of the covenant-relationship and acquires a 'righteousness' corresponding with them.

Paul agrees with regard to the content of the law. It *does* embody and express the will of God. It is 'righteous' (Rom. 7.12); and this moral righteousness must be embodied in the life of a man if there is to be that correspondence which the covenant-relationship and the status of *dikaiosynē* presupposes. So in 2.13 he insists 'It is not the hearers of the law who are righteous before God, but the doers of the law who shall be justified' (i.e., accepted as *dikaioi*). Indeed, the result of Christianity is not to abolish or change this moral content represented by the law, but precisely to enable people to embody its demands, to *fulfil* the law (8.4; 13.8).

The law declares well enough the quality of life which a man must have if he is to be capable of standing before God as 'righteous', but Paul's charge is that it is totally incapable of *effecting* that quality of life and therefore that standing. As a system of *making* men right with God it is a dead loss. It is powerless to produce the living that matches the righteousness of God. No one can be justified in the sight of God by works of the law (3.20). But neither certainly can they be justified by lawlessness. The situation seems hopeless.

But now a righteousness of God, which means both a righteousness *of* God and a righteousness *before* God, is revealed 'apart from law': it completely by-passes the law as a system of salvation. It is attested indeed by the law and the prophets – in its content it is in no sense inimical to them, as to be sure it cannot be since one is dealing with the same unchanging God. In fact Paul has just been quoting 'the law' (3.19) as a final confirmation of his case. Yet it is quite independent of law. It is a righteousness which comes *through* faith in Jesus Christ and *to* all who have such faith. This I believe to be the meaning of 'from faith ... to faith' in 1.17. It is not just a rhetorical phrase meaning 'a matter of faith from start to finish' (Dodd) or '*sola fide*' (Nygren). Justification is available on the basis of faith and is addressed to faith – and to all who have it. For there is no distinction; since all are sinners and 'go short' (rather than fall short) of the divine splendour which should be theirs. (For the meaning of this word, cf. Luke 15.15 of the prodigal son: he began to 'go short'.) But they are in the process of being justified free, gratis and for nothing by the sheer generosity of God through the act of emancipation or deliverance in Christ Jesus, where the background is probably not so much emancipation from slavery as God's archetypal deliverance of Israel from Egypt.

Finally, on the important words, faith (*pistis*) and its relation to justification. Properly speaking, we are not justified *by* faith, as though our faith were the instrument of our justification. This would only be another form of justification by works. We are justified by grace, on the basis of faith (*ek pisteōs*, 1.17; 3.26) or through faith (*dia pisteōs*, 3.22). The complete formula is 'by grace were you saved through faith; and that not of yourselves; it is the sheer gift of God' (Eph. 2.8).

'Not on the basis of works', goes on the passage in Ephesians. For faith is the opposite of any kind of earning or achievement. It is the correlative of sheer grace – utter receptiveness, bringing absolutely nothing in your hand, simply making room for God and his action, acknowledging there is nothing you can do or contribute. The archetype of faith for Paul is Abraham, who 'reckoned his own body as good as dead' (4.19) and simply threw himself in total trust upon the promise of God – 'giving the glory', attributing everything, 'to God'. It is *more* than this (positively it is faith-union with Christ); but this is where it starts, and it is on this basis that Paul propounds his gospel of justification, of a righteousness, a status before God, which has nothing to do with attainment or achievement.

Having now tried to define the basic categories – 'righteousness' on the one side and 'faith' on the other – let us see how Paul sees them as combining, through the life, death and resurrection of Jesus, to effect the *dikaiōsis* or setting right of the alienation between men and God which the law could not achieve. He is by no means always lucid, but the whole matter is a good deal simpler than later theology has often allowed it to appear.

We should do well to clear our minds at the outset of a righteousness either 'imparted' by some magical injection of grace or 'imputed' by some dubious legal fiction. The metaphor is indeed forensic – its home is in the law-courts – but its meaning for Paul the Christian can really be understood only if seen in terms of completely personal relationships. In fact the whole matter is now 'outside law': legal categories simply fail. The difficulty about Paul's language and what makes it so much more obscure than that of Jesus is that despite the fact that he says legal categories fail he goes on using legal categories, which inevitably do less than justice to and depersonalize the relationship he is trying to express. (On this cf. the excellent but critical discussion of justification in John Knox, *Chapters in a Life of Paul*, 1954, pp. 146–55.) The way Paul puts it, in terms of the courts rather than the family, may sometimes fail to convey the utterly personal relationship of repentance and forgiveness in terms of which Jesus spoke (these are two words Paul practically never uses), but fundamentally they were saying the same thing. Indeed, the whole Pauline doctrine is really contained in one verse of the parable of the pharisee and the publican (Luke 18.14): 'This man went down to his house *justified* rather than the other' – by sheerly throwing himself in penitent faith upon God and not by any record of merit. It does not mean, any more than in the case of the prodigal son, that God magically made him innocent or that he pretended by some legal fiction that he had no sin. It is simply that he was able to lift up his head, that God accepted him – and from that everything could follow:

43

'Accept the fact that you are accepted' (Tillich).

The difference is that Paul is writing the other side of the death and the resurrection of Christ, whereas Jesus was in the process of embodying the act of God which justified the ungodly, by his very attitude to publicans and sinners, by his free forgiveness of sins and bringing man to God on the basis of faith alone. Paul looks back on the whole *completed* act of God in Christ and sees it as the 'ransom' or 'redemption' which Jesus said it would be when perfected by his death (Mark 10.45; Rom. 3.24). In Jesus's blood (verse 25) – that is, in his life released through sacrifice (cf. Lev. 17.11) – he sees a great *hilastērion* or act of expiation for sin, to be appropriated through faith, by sheer acceptance and nothing else (not 'through faith in his blood', as in the 1662 Prayer Book prayer of oblation, but as a *hilastērion* in his blood or life).

For this important word *hilastērion* see Dodd, *The Bible and the Greeks*, 1935. chapter 5, or more briefly his *Romans, ad loc*. *Hilastērion* (and whether here it is a neuter noun, a mercy-seat, or a masculine adjective makes no real difference to the sense) is an instrument or place of the verb *hilaskesthai*. In non-biblical Greek this means (1) to placate or propitiate an angry person, especially a deity, and (2) to expiate sin or remove the taint of unholiness or taboo. The former of these meanings is much the more common. In biblical Greek (the LXX) the verb occurs about 110 times. Twice it is used of placating an angry man; three times of propitiating God (Zech. 7.2 and 8.22 of pagans propitiating the God of Israel and Mal. 1.9 in scornful irony). There is no other case of God being the object of the verb. Normally its object is the sin of man or that which is polluted by sin, e.g., altar or temple. There is a typical such use in Heb. 2.17: 'that he might be a merciful and faithful high priest before God, to expiate the sins of the people'. It means to perform an act by which the taint of sin is removed, to expiate. When God himself is the subject of the verb it not infrequently translates a Hebrew word meaning to 'forgive'. Cf. again the parable of the pharisee and the publican, where there is an analogous usage: 'God be merciful (*hilasthēti*) to me a sinner' (Luke 18.13).

44

Similarly in Paul it means to remove the taint of sin, not to propitiate God. For it is God who provides the *hilastērion*, not who is the object of it. It is that by which the power of sin is neutralized or disinfected, and therefore forgiven, and man is made fit for communion with the holy God. As B. F. Westcott put it, who anticipated much of this in his commentary on *The Epistles of St John*, 1883, pp. 83–85: 'The scriptural conception of *hilaskesthai* is not that of appeasing one who is angry, with a personal feeling, against the offender; but of altering the character of that which from without occasions a necessary alienation, and interposes an inevitable obstacle to fellowship'. This view has been contested, for instance by Leon Morris in his book *The Apostolic Preaching of the Cross* (1955). At the popular level the debate has been allowed to degenerate into a battle of words, with whether or not the term 'propitiation' is retained being seen as a sort of shibboleth or verbal test of sound doctrine. Certainly one may agree that the process neutralizes the 'wrath of God' (cf. Num. 16.46–48) *so long as* one remembers that this is not in Paul's thought to be regarded as assuaging an irate deity but as doing away with that alienation, that distortion in the personal relationship with God, which sin brings and which compels men to know God's love as wrath. The *hilastērion* does something not to God but to the sin which distorts and sours the relationship. By way of contrast I would cite something that I heard Billy Graham once say: 'The lightning of the divine justice struck Jesus instead of us.' The cross is here viewed as a lightning conductor which draws to itself the divine anger against sin and earths it. The *hilastērion* is then seen as neutralizing God's attitude rather than neutralizing the power and effect of sin – and this, with all due respect, is what is unbiblical, however many times it may be introduced with the rubric 'the Bible says'.

Perhaps this idea of neutralizing sin may provide some image for us of how Paul understood the work of Christ. For him the chief characteristic of Jesus's life and above all of his death was his 'obedience', which is his positive, and theologically admirable, way of asserting Jesus's sinlessness: e.g., Phil. 2.8, 'Christ

45

became obedient unto death even the death of the cross'; or Rom. 5.19, 'Through the obedience of the one man the many will be made righteous'. Paul sees Christ as going on by untiring obedience simply absorbing evil, soaking it up, refusing to pay it back or give it out, until on the cross he exhausts its power. There is nothing more that evil can do: it is simply finished, and still it has not conquered him in the only way evil can really conquer a man, that is by making him evil. In some such way as this Paul sees Christ, in his life and above all in his sacrificial death, neutralizing the power of sin, acting as he puts it, in one of his rare uses of sacrificial categories, as an expiation. Or perhaps we could put it in medical categories: as an antiseptic, taking the sepsis out of the system so that the God-given healing processes can do their proper priest-like work of restoring what Peter in Acts describes as 'perfect soundness' (3.16). And, Paul's gospel goes on, anyone who in sheer faith and trust accepts what Christ has done and lets this restorative power into his own life, who dies to sin in his obedience, by being crucified with him and joined to his life-giving body, is accepted by God and is 'right' with him, be he never so hopeless a sinner.

But all this last carries us well beyond the stage Paul has so far reached. He is not in chapter 3 concerned with our appropriation. He is content to say that this new right-standing is open to all on the ground of faith, without yet elaborating faith in its fullness as faith-union with Christ or speaking of the life-giving powers of the Spirit. At this point he is concerned simply with the objective thing that God has done in Christ, which he describes as his act of righteousness, or way of righting wrong. And he proceeds to show *how* and in what sense it *is* a 'demonstration' of God's righteousness. Such a demonstration, he says (verse 25b), is necessary and indeed overdue. The forbearance of God with sin in the past, which is another theme common to Romans and Acts 17 (cf. the 'overlooking' of the times of ignorance in 17.30), has impugned the seriousness with which God may be supposed to take sin. It has caused men to think (Rom. 2.4) precisely what is suggested by the Psalmist when he makes God say: 'These things you have done and I have been silent; you thought that I was one like yourself' (50.21). Moreover, a demonstration that God does not sacrifice moral realities is even more necessary if, as Paul asserts, he actually justifies the wicked – for that, as the Proverb says, is 'an abomination to the Lord'.

So Paul seeks to show (verse 26) that the act of redemption in Christ really is a demonstration of God's righteousness, and that in two senses:

(a) It does demonstrate that he himself is just, that he is vindicated as *holy* love and does not palter with sin. For, if this act of justification is given free, gratis and for nothing it certainly does not cost God nothing: it costs the life of his Son (cf. 8.32, 'he did not spare his own Son'). Moreover it is a real *hilastērion*: it does deal with sin, it does not just by-pass it – forgiving by forgetting – but neutralizes it by obedience. Further, as he will go on to show in chapter 6, faith in Christ through which a man is justified is no fiction but a real self-identification (in baptism) with his death to sin, and nothing less. It does not allow us to continue in sin (6.1). God does take sin very seriously. He *can* do all this without his hatred of it being called in question. That is a vital point for Paul, and one of the most difficult he had to establish. God is, and must be, 'himself just'.

But (b) this act of righteousness is no mere sterile demonstration that God himself is just, that he hates sin. The prophets and the priests had said that. It is a demonstration that he does something creative about sin – that despite being of purer eyes than to behold iniquity, he reaches through to the sinner and sets him in the right. He is a just God and a saviour, 'just and justifying'. The human situation was such that up till then it seemed that he could not justify men and be *holy* love – that his righteousness could not go forth and bestow acceptance on the other of what the Fourth Gospel calls 'the right to be called the children of God' (John 1.12). But 'now in this present time', picking up the emphatic 'but now' in verse 21, it has gone forth: it has been and is being revealed, a new and living way has been opened up, as the epistle to the Hebrews puts it (10.20).

Romans 3.21–26 is the most concentrated and heavily theological summary of the Pauline gospel, and every word has to be wrestled with. But if we take the trouble it demands and really enter into the background of his words it is not, I believe, obscure, however profound. So much doubtful theology has been built up on it. It has been associated with false or one-sided ideas of propitiation, satisfaction and penal substitution. Indeed I would want to question both words in that last particular shibboleth. The New Testament *never* says that God punishes Christ: in fact the verb and noun for 'punishment' are only used twice each in the whole of the New Testament, and never of God or Christ. Moreover, Christ stands as our representative, not as our replacement. Except in Mark 10.45, where it is part of the ransom metaphor, his work is always on behalf of us (*hyper*) not instead of us (*anti*). Of course Christ does something we could never do for ourselves. He is there because we are not. But he died to sin not so that we shall not have to (as our substitute) but precisely so that we can (as our representative). On the subtle and profound difference between these two, cf. D. Sölle, *Christ the Representative*, 1967.

All such distortion and polarization – now happily healed, over justification, which split the church in the sixteenth century – need never have happened if a truly critical theological approach had been available. This passage by itself almost provides a sufficient vindication of the value of sound theology to the church! So I make no apology for having given it such an extended amount of space.

27   What room then is left for human pride? It is excluded. And on what principle? The keeping of the law would not exclude it, but
28   faith does. For our argument is that a man is justified by faith quite apart from success in keeping the law.

29   Do you suppose God is the God of the Jews alone? Is he not
30   the God of Gentiles also? Certainly, of Gentiles also, if it be true that God is one. And he will therefore justify both the circumcised in virtue of their faith, and the uncircumcised through their
31   faith. Does this mean that we are using faith to undermine law? By no means: we are placing law itself on a firmer footing.

Verse 27. Here we have a good example of the very broad, and often slippery, use of the word *nomos* (law) by Paul. Here he uses it in the secular Greek sense of 'principle'. Achievement would not exclude pride; but faith does, because faith is sheer. self-emptying, the admission of absolute inability to do anything in one's own strength.

Verse 28. Notice the present tense, 'is, or is being, justified', as earlier in verse 24. This does not mean that justification is not a once for all act. Yet it is not *only* this, but also a process thus initiated. It is important to stress this only because it is constantly denied. Justification is said to be the initial act, sanctification the subsequent process. But there is no basis in Paul for this later ecclesiastical schematization. Justification and sanctification, indeed like all the great words for salvation, are both past, present and future – an act accomplished, a process being worked out, a consummation yet awaited. Thus the verb to 'justify', confining ourselves to Romans, is used in the past (5.1, 9), present (3.24, 28) and the future (2.13; 3.30); while the terms for 'sanctification', rare in Romans, refer to the past in I Cor. 1.30; 6.11, to the present in I Thess. 4.3–4; II Cor. 7.1 and to the future in I Thess. 5.23; II Cor. 7.1. The difference is simply that one, justification, is expressed in terms of forensic metaphors and speaks of the communication of God's righteousness to sinners, whereas the other, sanctification, works with sacrificial metaphors and speaks of the communication of God's holiness to sinners. To elaborate this would take us too far from Romans, for in this epistle Paul is working almost exclusively with the forensic metaphor and hardly uses the other, though he mixes them interestingly in 6.15–23, especially in verse 19: 'Yield your bodies as slaves to righteousness unto sanctification.'

Verse 29. 'Or do you really imagine God is the God of the Jews only?' – as he would be if salvation were by the law alone. But the most fundamental Jewish doctrine, that God is one, means that he must be the God of the Gentiles as well. Being a true Jew therefore itself implies that salvation cannot be exclusive, that it cannot be by the law alone. This is in fact the position of modern Judaism. The Jew says that the law is God's way for him, but he does not insist that it is God's way for everyone. Judaism has accepted the force of Paul's logic at this point, that if God is one salvation cannot be by the law alone. But it has not accepted his further and more radical conclusion, that it cannot be by the law at all. As T. W. Manson has put it, if the question posed in the epistle is: 'Can one be a good Christian without embracing Judaism?', Paul's answer is to throw back the question: 'Can one be a good Jew without embracing Christianity?'

Verse 30. Paul uses two parallel expressions, 'of faith' (*ek pisteōs*) and 'through faith' (*dia tēs pisteōs*). It may be a purely stylistic variation or rhetorical device, as many commentators have asserted. But why does he go out of his way to make the repetition at all? There is truth in Lightfoot's contention (*Notes on Epistles of St Paul*, 1895, p. 274) that the difference can be seen by transposing the proposition into the negative. God will not justify the circumcision *ek nomou*, on the ground of the law, because they have the law, and he will not justify the uncircumcision *dia tou nomou*, by putting them through the law, i.e., by making them become Jews (as Judaism assumed). In his lectures on Romans at Cambridge a century ago Lightfoot put it thus: 'When speaking of Jews the point is the falseness of their *starting point*, from the law and not from faith. With Gentiles the point is the needlessness of a new *instrumentality*. They start from faith and have no need to call in the intervention of the law'. He cites Origen, saying 'the Greek fathers knew what the language meant': 'We must not suppose that he used the prepositions at random', and he quotes I Cor. 11.12: 'If the woman was made out of (*ek*) man, it is through (*dia*) woman that man comes to be.' And this difference is confirmed below in Rom. 4.11–16, where there is the same distinction between the two prepositions. It is a good example of how, if we dig into Paul, he is seldom found to use words casually.

Verse 31. Well then, do we annul law through faith? Not for one moment. We actually (*alla*) put it on a firmer footing. 'What rubbish!', I remember Dodd exclaiming at this point when we were translating the New English Bible. But to understand Paul we must remember that he is constantly regarding the law from two points of view, which he does not always clearly distinguish: (1) as embodying the content of the will of God; and (2) as a way of putting men right with God, a system of salvation. In fact, the law as (2) he *has* completely annulled. The law as (1) he refuses to annul, and in fact goes on to show that only the Christian can really fulfil it. If he had used, say, 'the commandment' for (1), the moral content of the will of God, and 'works' for (2), the technique of salvation, he would have saved himself from much apparent inconsistency. As a Jew, he cannot 'abolish the law' simply like that, for it is 'holy', it is 'spiritual' (7.12, 14). Yet in Eph. 2.15 he represents Christ on the cross precisely as having 'abolished the law', the law however here being viewed not as spiritual but actually as 'the enmity', the symbol of division and alienation between Jew and Gentile. As such, as an exclusive system of salvation, it is absolutely out. It is important to see that this is the real distinction and not, as Dodd suggests, that Paul distinguishes between the legal side of Jewish religion and the prophetic side (which he also calls 'the law'), and that while he was quite willing to treat the former as expendable he refused, unlike Marcion, to throw out the whole of the Old Testament.

But more on the law later. Notice how Paul trails his coat on the subject of the law. In 3.20 he propounded the unsupported thesis: 'No human being can be justified in the sight of God for having kept the law: law brings only the consciousness of sin.' Here in 3.31 he does the same: 'Does this mean we are using faith to undermine the law? By no means: we are placing law itself on a firmer footing.' Both of these theses he throws out and leaves – to be taken up later.

Meanwhile he launches on an excursus (chapter 4) to meet the Jewish objection, that Abraham, the natural ancestor of the race and the type of all that was to follow, could indeed plead privilege and merit. What was God meaning with Abraham? What do you make of him? Paul sees this as the crucial case, and he tackles it on the objector's own ground and with his weapons. Abraham in fact, says Paul, illustrates his point rather than denies it.

4 What, then, are we to say about Abraham, our ancestor in the
2 natural line? If Abraham was justified by anything he had done,
   then he has a ground for pride. But he has no such ground before
3 God; for what does Scripture say? 'Abraham put his faith in
4 God, and that faith was counted to him as righteousness.' Now if
   a man does a piece of work, his wages are not 'counted' as a
5 favour; they are paid as debt. But if without any work to his
   credit he simply puts his faith in him who acquits the guilty, then
6 his faith is indeed 'counted as righteousness'. In the same sense
   David speaks of the happiness of the man whom God 'counts' as
7 just, apart from any specific acts of justice: 'Happy are they', he
   says, 'whose lawless deeds are forgiven, whose sins are buried
8 away; happy is the man whose sins the Lord does not count
9 against him.' Is this happiness confined to the circumcised, or is it
   for the uncircumcised also? Consider: we say, 'Abraham's faith
10 was counted as righteousness'; in what circumstances was it so

11 counted? Was he circumcised at the time, or not? He was not yet circumcised, but uncircumcised; and he later received the symbolic rite of circumcision as the hallmark of the righteousness which faith had given him when he was still uncircumcised. Con-

12 sequently, he is the father of all who have faith when uncircumcised, so that righteousness is 'counted' to them; and at the same time he is the father of such of the circumcised as do not rely upon their circumcision alone, but also walk in the footprints of the faith which our father Abraham had while he was yet uncircumcised.

13 For it was not through law that Abraham, or his posterity, was given the promise that the world should be his inheritance, but

14 through the righteousness that came from faith. For if those who hold by the law, and they alone, are heirs, then faith is empty and

15 the promise goes for nothing, because law can bring only retribution; but where there is no law there can be no breach of law.

16 The promise was made on the ground of faith, in order that it might be a matter of sheer grace, and that it might be valid for all Abraham's posterity, not only for those who hold by the law, but for those also who have the faith of Abraham. For he is the

17 father of us all, as Scripture says: 'I have appointed you to be father of many nations.' This promise, then, was valid before God, the God in whom he put his faith, the God who makes the dead live and summons things that are not yet in existence as if

18 they already were. When hope seemed hopeless, his faith was such that he became 'father of many nations', in agreement with the words which had been spoken to him: 'Thus shall your post-

19 erity be.' Without any weakening of faith he contemplated his own body, as good as dead (for he was about a hundred years

20 old), and the deadness of Sarah's womb, and never doubted

21 God's promise, but, strong in faith, gave honour to God, in the

22 firm conviction of his power to do what he had promised. And that is why Abraham's faith was 'counted to him as righteousness'.

23 24 Those words were written, not for Abraham's sake alone, but for our sake too: it is to be 'counted' in the same way to us who have faith in the God who raised Jesus our Lord from the dead;

25 for he was delivered to death for our misdeeds, and raised to life to justify us.[a]

a. *Or* raised to life because we were now justified.

His argument is that scripture proves his case in two ways:
(*a*) (verses 2–8) by its very use of this word 'counted' or 'reckoned' (Gen. 15.6). For what you *earn* cannot be described as
counted as a favour. He may stress the implications of the word
because the current Jewish interpretation of this passage was in
exactly the opposite direction. Thus I Macc. 2.51–52 includes
under 'the deeds of the fathers' the illustration, 'Did not
Abraham prove steadfast under trial and so gain credit as a
righteous man?' But this clearly refers to Abraham's willingness
to sacrifice Isaac – an illustration which Paul noticeably avoids.
(*b*) (verses 9–12) by the fact that this statement (Gen. 15.6)
comes before, not after, any reference to circumcision (Gen.
17.10–14), and therefore his acceptance by God does not
depend on circumcision. This is a very palpable hit. And, as
Dodd points out, this sequence is still valid for us with our
critical approach to the Old Testament: 'The early-prophetic
stories of Abraham know nothing of his circumcision, which is
mentioned only in the late priestly document.'

In the parallel discussion of Gal. 3.6–9, as in Rom. 4.17 below, Paul stresses the fact that the promise to Abraham was that
he should be the father of *many* nations, and not of the Jewish
people only. So here (verse 11), since Abraham's faith is the
fundamental thing (circumcision being merely the confirmatory
seal of God's authentication), the true descendants of Abraham
are those who are in the succession of his faith, not of his circumcision only.

Verses 13–15. As the promise to Abraham was not dependent on circumcision, so it was not dependent on the law. Here
Paul summarizes his argument of Gal. 3.10–14. He does not, as
in Gal. 3.17, go on to show, as he well might have, that the
promise (Gen. 17.5) is not only prior in time to circumcision
(Gen. 17.10–14) but is prior to the law by the whole 430 years
which on his chronology separated Abraham from Moses.
(Here incidentally Dodd again shows well how this may be
interpreted in terms of our modern understanding of the Old
Testament. Most of the stories of Abraham belong to that
stratum of the Pentateuch (JE) which took form under the

influence of the earlier prophets and belong to a stage of Hebrew religion which was as a matter of fact about four centuries prior to the new legalism of the post-exilic period, represented by P.) But here in Romans Paul employs the argument not of historical priority, the *later* law cannot annul the covenant of promise, but of logical incompatibility. 'Law' is the antithesis of 'promise'. There is no point in speaking of 'faith' or 'promise' at all, if being right with God is a matter of working your passage home.

But Paul cannot mention the law without trailing his coat. Once again in verse 15 he throws out a pithy aphorism, which he leaves for justification till later: 'Law can only bring retribution (*orgē*); but where there is no law there can be no breach of law (*parabasis*).'

In verses 16–25 Abraham's faith is seen as a type of the Christian's. It is the abandonment of any human confidence, hope or power – trusting utterly to the promise and power of God, being absolutely open and disposable for him. It is 'giving honour to God', ascribing everything to him. This is a Hebraism: cf. Josh. 7.19 (of Achan), John 9.24 (of the man born blind) and Acts 12.23 (of Herod). Note that the example of Abraham's faith which Paul takes is not, as I said earlier, his sacrifice of Isaac (as in James and the epistle to the Hebrews) – this would be dangerously near to 'works' – but God's ability for creation *ex nihilo*. When there seemed no future, God raised posterity for him as it were from the dead. So faith for Paul, when it is not, as it usually is, faith in Christ, is faith in God who raises from the dead. The justifying faith of the Christian is therefore of the same quality as that of Abraham.

Verse 25, 'He was delivered to death for our misdeeds, and raised to life for our justification', is a typical Pauline doctrinal summary introduced *en passant* and tacked on by a relative pronoun. Clearly there is no separation or antithesis intended here between the cross and resurrection. It is a characteristic piece of Hebrew poetic parallelism – he died and rose for our justification from sin – and could well reflect the rhythm of a primitive hymn or credal formula. The whole thing constitutes the act of 'setting right', not merely the resurrection. Indeed in 5.9 it is 'the blood' by which we are justified – that is, as in 3.25, the life released through death.

5.1–11

---

5   Therefore, now that we have been justified through faith, let us continue at peace[a] with God through our Lord Jesus Christ,
2   through whom we have been allowed to enter the sphere of God's grace, where we now stand. Let us exult[b] in the hope of
3   the divine splendour that is to be ours. More than this: let us even exult[c] in our present sufferings, because we know that suf-
4   fering trains us to endure, and endurance brings proof that we
5   have stood the test, and this proof is the ground of hope. Such a hope is no mockery, because God's love has flooded our inmost heart through the Holy Spirit he has given us.
6   For at the very time when we were still powerless, then Christ
7   died for the wicked. Even for a just man one of us would hardly die, though perhaps for a good man one might actually brave
8   death; but Christ died for us while we were yet sinners, and that
9   is God's own proof of his love towards us. And so, since we have now been justified by Christ's sacrificial death, we shall all the
10   more certainly be saved through him from final retribution. For if, when we were God's enemies, we were reconciled to him through the death of his Son, much more, now that we are recon-
11   ciled, shall we be saved by his life. But that is not all: we also exult in God through our Lord Jesus, through whom we have now been granted reconciliation.

a. *Some witnesses read* we are at peace.
b. *Or* We exult.
c. *Or* We even exult.

Paul now goes on to dilate in triumph upon the expansive new life which is open to the person who has passed through the narrow gate of justification by faith. It is indeed 'life from the dead'. Here are sketched the themes which will occupy the second half of the doctrinal section of the epistle and as though in an overture to Act II the tunes are played over. The new words are peace, glory, endurance, hope, love, the Spirit, salvation, reconciliation, life. They are all given their full orchestration and reach their crescendo in chapter 8. These verses, which raise the argument to a new level, are to chapter 8 what 1.16–17 were to chapter 3, where the key words were 'to Jew first and also to Greek, righteousness, faith'.

Verse 1. There is a textual crux at this point. There are two readings, 'we have (*echomen*) peace' and 'let us have (*echōmen*) peace'. The manuscript evidence is overwhelmingly in favour of the latter, though many commentators are so convinced that exhortation is out of place that they prefer the indicative nevertheless, adducing other examples of the long and short 'o' being confused. A very convincing example of this is I Cor. 15.49, where the manuscript evidence is overwhelmingly in favour of *phoresōmen* ('let us wear'), where the sense clearly requires *phoresomen*, 'as we have worn the image of the earthly so we shall wear the image of the heavenly'.) So here the RSV opts for the indicative. We must remember that Paul dictated the epistle (16.22) and it is quite possible that Tertius misheard what would have been a very slight difference in pronunciation. We always assume that the original manuscript, if we could but establish it, would be without slip. But this is not true of any letter of any length that I have ever written. I am inclined to think that the autograph may well have had the subjunctive *echōmen* but that Paul would have been the first to amend it. In other words the indicative is a scribal correction, but a correct one. Yet there is really no means of proving that Paul did not write and could not have meant 'let us enjoy the peace' (Moffatt) or 'let us continue at peace' (NEB).

Verse 2, 'We have been allowed to enter'. *Prosagōgē*, used also in Eph. 2.18 and 3.12, describes the access which comes of accepting the fact that we are accepted. The prodigal son has been allowed to enter a new status, where henceforth everything is different. Everything can now be enjoyed as a son.

Notice the contrast between the complete exclusion of 'boasting' in 3.27 and the Christian 'boasting'. It is the same distinction that Paul makes elsewhere between 'glorying in the flesh' and 'glorying in the Lord'.

'The divine splendour which is to be ours'. This is the restoration of that transfiguring of human nature by the divine which for the Rabbis was characteristic of man in paradise and of which he now goes short (3.23). We have the same promise of the ultimate destiny of the people of God in the Qumran Manual of Discipline: 'For God has chosen them for an eternal covenant so that theirs is all the glory of Adam' (1QS 4.23). 'Glory' (*doxa*) is an eschatological word, and, as in every other such case, it is characteristic that Paul should speak of it both as an accomplished fact for Christians (Rom. 8.30, 'he has glorified us') and as a present possession (II Cor. 3.18, 'we reflect the glory of the Lord') and as a future hope (here and in Rom. 8.17–18, 'that we may be glorified', 'the glory that will be revealed'). The whole process is summed up in II Cor. 3.18, where Paul says that we are being transformed 'from glory to glory', which probably means not simply that we are growing in glory, but 'from the glory we have received to the glory that will be ours'. The whole Christian life is built upon the pattern of 'become what you are': all things are yours – all is to be made yours. Perhaps the same pattern is to be seen in II Cor. 2.16, where the Christian life is described as 'from life to life'.

Verse 5. God's love *has* flooded our hearts through the Holy Spirit which *was* given to us. Here is the same combination of the once and for all and the continuing. The words are a fulfilment of Isa. 44.3: 'I will pour water upon him that is thirsty, and streams upon the dry ground: I will pour my Spirit upon thy seed.' Compare I Cor. 12.13: 'In one Spirit we were all baptised into one body ... and were all made to drink of one Spirit.' Note that the water metaphor is one of irrigation rather than of washing (of which there is surprisingly little mention in Paul, for whom baptism is primarily a 'burial').

Verses 6–8 represent the charter of the Christian's salvation – the incredible basic fact upon which all the boundless benefits of the new life rest. To these Paul returns in verses 9–11 with two *a fortiori* arguments introduced by the words 'how much more' and depending on the premise 'while we were yet sinners'. If such grace was shown to us *then*, how much more *now* that we have been accepted as *dikaioi*. The contrast between the 'just man' and the 'good man' is, as Lightfoot pointed out, classical rather than Hebraic.

In verse 9 once again we meet the *orgē*, the final retribution, which is already at work proleptically in history. This is a good example of its impersonal use: literally, 'saved through him from the wrath'. It is not God's anger in contrast with his love, which would make Paul's argument meaningless. Indeed God's love is the subject of the whole process.

Verse 10. The same process of justification is now expressed in the metaphor not of the law courts but of reconciliation after estrangement. Reconciliation is not (as with us) the last stage in forgiveness, but yet another metaphor for stating the fact of a lost status restored, access re-opened. It is an initial past act of God leading like everything else into a continuing process: cf. II Cor. 5.18–20: 'From first to last this has been the work of God. He has reconciled us men to himself through Christ. . . . In Christ's name, we implore you, be reconciled to God!' The future state here in verse 10 is expressed in terms of being 'saved' – though this is equally a past fact (Rom. 8.24) and a present experience (I Cor. 1.18). This again only goes to show that, while Paul certainly did think of the Christian life as a process from a *fait accompli* to a future completion, none of his words can be tied to any one stage in that process (e.g., that we have been justified, we are being sanctified, we shall be saved). Any word may be used of any stage according to what aspect of it he wishes to bring out.

Now, after the bridge-passage that introduces the great themes of the new life in chapters 5–8, Paul takes up his argument again. The structure is the same as before: 1.16–17 = 5.1–11 (playing over the theme); 1.18–3.20 = 5.12–7.25 (establishing the negative); 3.21–4.25 = 8.1–39 (expounding the positive).

12 Mark what follows. It was through one man that sin entered the world, and through sin death, and thus death pervaded the whole
13 human race, inasmuch as all men have sinned. For sin was already in the world before there was law, though in the absence
14 of law no reckoning is kept of sin. But death held sway from Adam to Moses, even over those who had not sinned as Adam did, by disobeying a direct command – and Adam foreshadows the Man who was to come.

15 But God's act of grace is out of all proportion to Adam's wrongdoing. For if the wrongdoing of that one man brought death upon so many, its effect is vastly exceeded by the grace of God and the gift that came to so many by the grace of the one
16 man, Jesus Christ. And again, the gift of God is not to be compared in its effect with that one man's sin; for the judicial action, following upon the one offence, issued in a verdict of condemnation, but the act of grace, following upon so many misdeeds,
17 issued in a verdict of acquittal. For if by the wrongdoing of that one man death established its reign, through a single sinner, much more shall those who receive in far greater measure God's grace, and his gift of righteousness, live and reign through the one man, Jesus Christ.

18 It follows, then, that as the issue of one misdeed was condemnation for all men, so the issue of one just act is acquittal and life
19 for all men. For as through the disobedience of the one man the many were made sinners, so through the obedience of the one man the many will be made righteous.

20 Law intruded into this process to multiply law-breaking. But
21 where sin was thus multiplied, grace immeasurably exceeded it, in order that, as sin established its reign by way of death, so God's grace might establish its reign in righteousness, and issue in eternal life through Jesus Christ our Lord.

In the first stage of the argument Paul expounded his doctrine of the universal justification through faith after establishing the universality of wrath or alienation as the result of sin. Now he goes on to expound the state that is opened up by justification, the universal life that is available to every man in Christ. But for this he must first establish the universality of death as the result of sin; and there is a real parallelism in his argument. Just as the condition of sin and wrath is universal without distinction, whether men have the advantage of the law or not, so the condition of sin and death is universal, for all the sons of Adam, even over those who did not have the law of Moses. In fact the distinction introduced by law is irrelevant as far as death is concerned, just as it was irrelevant in the case of sin. Its intrusion (verse 20) makes a difference indeed to the degree of guilt, but not to the universality of death (verse 13). Death knows no distinctions, and the universality of *death* is the point that Paul is here concerned with. He is not propounding, as he has often been taken to be doing, a doctrine of original *sin* for its own sake, which can be said to be distinctively Christian and indeed distinctively Pauline. In fact he is here simply taking over accepted doctrine of late Judaism, which had already grounded the universality of death in the universality of sin. We are at liberty to modify that understanding of the *cause* of death and its precise nexus with sin (and more of that below), without destroying Paul's fundamental argument: 'Death is *universal* outside Christ: life is available to all in Christ'. In this argument there are two stages:

(*a*) 'Through one man ... sin.' This was current Jewish teaching: through the fall of Adam all men fell into sin. Cf. again II Esdras: 'For the first man, Adam, burdened with an evil heart, transgressed and was overcome, as were also all those who were descended from him. Thus the disease became permanent: the law was in the people's heart along with the evil root, but what was good departed, and the evil remained' (3.21–22; cf. 4.30; 7.48). There is nothing new in what Paul is saying, and his point does not depend on accepting the historicity of Adam as a datable individual. In fact it is quite possible that like Philo and other educated Jews of the time he would have accepted the Adam story as we should as an allegory or myth. In any case what he is saying about the universality and solidarity of sin is independent of any literalism, and is abun-

61

dantly verified by experience. Sin is there before us: we are formed to personality, brought to moral consciousness, in and through a social order which is already self-centred rather than God-centred. Therefore we are called into a personal existence which is distorted before ever we make a conscious moral judgment; we are brought up by imitation and reaction to look after number one. And however far we go back in history that is true of every person born into this world alive. Sin is not an individual phenomenon which it just happens that everyone 'gets' (like measles), although they might not. It is woven into the very texture of humanity as we know it, so that we are not like Adam in the myth perfectly free to choose *either* good *or* evil. There is a unity and solidarity in sin which can be expressed by saying not merely that all men are sinners but that man is a sinner. In this matter one can talk of humanity as one man – in terms of Man (Adam) without any fear that one's generalization will be wrong; cf. II Esd. 8.35: 'The truth is, no man was ever born who did not sin; no man alive is innocent of offence.' It is this *fact* of experience, as true in the twentieth century as in the first, of which Paul is speaking.

(*b*) 'Through sin death.' This again is nothing new. It is not stated in Genesis 3 that Adam would have been immortal apart from sin, although the second half of the description of man, 'Dust you are, *to dust you shall return*' (3.19), could be read as a word of judgment. But in any case contemporary Judaism under Greek influence saw man as originally created for an immortality lost through sin. Cf. Wisd. 2.23–24: 'God created man for immortality and made him the image of his own eternal self; it was the devil's spite that brought death into the world', and II Esd. 3.7: 'You gave him [Adam] your one commandment to obey; he disobeyed it, and thereupon you made him subject to death, him and his descendants.'

Paul is here including the purely biological fact of dying as part of the consequences of sin, which, with our knowledge of evolution is for us impossible. Death was a biological fact on earth long before sin was a moral fact. But we can make the distinction, which he did not need to, between death as a purely organic, animal fact and the death of *man*, which is always also a spiritual fact, including as it does the consciousness and fear of death. Cf. II Esd. 7[64] contrasting the death of man with that of the beasts: 'But ... we grow up with the power of thought and are tortured by it; we are doomed to die and we know it.' The distinctive thing about human death, to which a secular existentialist like Heidegger bore equal testimony, is that death comes to man as something for which he was *not* made, as an offence, cutting short and reducing to meaninglessness all that is highest and distinctive about him, the negation of love and his personal existence and values. The Hebrews had this under- standing of man's death as a deeply spiritual phenomenon developed in high degree – corresponding to their high doctrine of man as made in the image of God. That the beasts should perish was natural; that man should be doomed to an end like theirs was profoundly unnatural. It was a sign of a deep-seated aberrance in things – or rather in man, though the effect of spiritual forces outside man was not excluded. Indeed death itself in late Judaism, as in Paul, is personified as a spiritual power (in I Cor. 15.54–56, as in this passage). It is the embodi- ment *par excellence* of the spirit-forces of evil, the 'world rul- ers'; it is the last enemy (I Cor. 15.26). Or, looked at more impersonally, death is the end-term, the fruit, the wages, of the consequences of sin, both physical and spiritual. It is the final climax to which *echthra* (enmity or alienation) and *orgē* (wrath) lead. In the same way for Paul life is the end-term of 'righteous- ness' and 'sanctification'. The parallelism is important for him, and surely valid for us. Death for man is not purely a biological, but a spiritual fact; and we cannot separate the physical and the spiritual. Death as a doom is the seal and sacrament of sin. That in modern terms is what Paul is saying.

But for his present argument the important point is the utter *universality* of death. Man, again, is one in this. Death over- spreads the whole human situation – inasmuch as all have sin- ned. For all have made their own what Adam did. He is truly depicted therefore in the story as representative man. Note es- pecially the 'inasmuch as' (*eph' hō(i)*) all have sinned, *not*, as

Augustine disastrously concluded from the ambiguity of the Vulgate's *in quo*, 'in whom', in whose loins, all succeeding men were willy-nilly involved in sinning by mere biological descent. The Greek is unambiguous and does not eliminate moral responsibility.

In verses 13–14 Paul goes on to make the important point that sin (*hamartia*) is not merely, as Pelagian Englishmen tend to assume, a conscious act of individual wrong-doing ('a sin' – though he can talk about 'sins' when he wants to, as in 4.7 and 5.16). It is an objective and corporate condition of having-gone-wrongness, of having missed the mark, got off-centre, which means that man lacks the crowning glory, the true divine humanity, which should be his. This is a universal fact, common to all men. And it is this objective condition of which death is the end-term, whether a man is fully *aware* of what wrong is or not. Consciousness of sin, and therefore guilt, enters only when there is a recognized norm or standard which you know you are flouting. And, says Paul, sin was in the world before this – or, as we might put it, sin, the objective fact of being off-centre, of missing the mark, is to be found in every individual and every society prior even to the time when that individual or society comes to the level of moral consciousness and responsibility. Paul thinks of this awareness of a norm, for the Jew at any rate (though contrast 2.14), as a datable fact in history – the revelation of the law through Moses. And in a real sense this *was* the point when the Jews came to national self-consciousness as a people and bound themselves in a specific moral relationship to Yahweh, saying, 'All these things will we do' (Exod. 24.3–8).

It is at this point that sin in general (*hamartia*) can come to have the nature of *parabasis*, law-breaking, transgression of a known command. But Paul is faced with a difficulty. For Adam was guilty of *parabasis* long before this moment, since he was clearly confronted in the Garden with a command of God and knew that he was disobeying him. Paul's answer is to see this consciousness of sin's true nature, and therefore the possibility of *parabasis*, as having been lost through sin itself, till it was reintroduced in the Mosaic law. And it is possible (I think it is probable, though no one else seems to!) that the clause in verse 14, 'who is the type of him who was to come', is introduced in recognition that there is here a real difficulty. How could Adam be guilty of transgression before the law? Answer: he represents a type or prefigurement of the man or situation that was to come, i.e., man under the law. Or, as we might put it, he is not typical of man prior to the law (indeed there he stands alone), but he is typical of the man of the future, Mosaic man, or perhaps simply 'the future' (*tou mellontos* in the neuter being the regular Greek for 'the future'). This at least gives a very good meaning to the clause and a reason for its being there – to meet the implied difficulty of Adam not being a real type: his immediate successors did *not* sin as he did.

But the regular interpretation is to make this clause purely resumptive, to get the argument back on to the lines from which it is by now getting hopelessly side-tracked. In fact the sentence never ends. It started with a comparison, 'as through one man', implying 'so through one man'. But the course of the argument has become complicated by this tiresome intruder the law – and it is an intruder because, as Paul says, whether man is under law or not does not make any difference to the universality of death, though it is important to say this. So now, it is maintained, he gets back by a transitional clause: 'and Adam foreshadows the Man (Christ) who was to come'.

But even then he does not get back on to the same lines. In fact it is not so much a comparison as a contrast (verse 15), or rather it is a comparison which breaks down, because the second limb is incomparably the more wonderful. The exact contrast is not easy to pin down – Paul's ideas tumble over one another. It is in general that the grace available, being of God, is so much the greater in its power and effects than the sin, which is of man. But there is the supplementary contrast in verse 16, that whereas the legal action (*krima*) (as in I Cor. 6.7, 'You have lawsuits (*krimata*) between yourselves') brought about all this retribution for only one offence, God's gracious action (*charisma*) started from innumerable offences. It should therefore in justice have meted out all the more wrath, and this is what makes its verdict of acquittal the more wonderful. But this contrast mixes somewhat confusedly with the underlying point of *comparison* (to which he finally returns in verses 18–19) that both these effects came through one man, the representative man Adam and the representative man Jesus Christ.

Verse 19. 'The many were made, or constituted, sinners ... the many will be made, or constituted, righteous.' The verb means to make (cf. Acts 7.27, 'Who made you a ruler and judge over us?') not merely to count. Certainly we are not merely 'counted' sinners. 'But', comments Barrett, 'the words "sinners" and "righteous" are words of relationship, not character. Adam's disobedience did not mean that all men necessarily and without their consent committed particular acts of sin; it meant that they were born into a race which had separated itself from God. Similarly, Christ's obedience did not mean that henceforth men did nothing but righteous acts, but that in Christ they were related to God as Christ himself was related to his Father.'

Verse 20. 'Law intruded into this process to multiply law-breaking': another *obiter dictum* on the subject of the law which Paul will take up with the others in chapter 7. For him the law is parenthetic (*pareisēlthen*) not only to his argument here but to the whole dispensation of grace and faith. For this is the normative relation between God and man and exists on both sides of the bracket of the law-works relationship, a bracket which had to be inserted in order to bring home the real sinfulness of sin.

Verse 21. Literally, 'through righteousness ... to life'. This sums up the whole movement of Paul's argument in the two parts of the first half of the epistle (1–4; 5–8).

6   What are we to say, then? Shall we persist in sin, so that there
2   may be all the more grace? No, no! We died to sin: how can we
3   live in it any longer? Have you forgotten that when we were
    baptized into union with Christ Jesus we were baptized into his
4   death? By baptism we were buried with him, and lay dead, in
    order that, as Christ was raised from the dead in the splendour of
    the Father, so also we might set our feet upon the new path of
    life.

5   For if we have become incorporate with him in a death like his,
6   we shall also be one with him in a resurrection like his. We know
    that the man we once were has been crucified with Christ, for the
    destruction of the sinful self, so that we may no longer be the
7   slaves of sin, since a dead man is no longer answerable for his sin.
8   But if we thus died with Christ, we believe that we shall also
9   come to life with him. We know that Christ, once raised from the
    dead, is never to die again: he is no longer under the dominion of
10 death. For in dying as he died, he died to sin, once for all, and in
11 living as he lives, he lives to God. In the same way you must
    regard yourselves as dead to sin and alive to God, in union with
    Christ Jesus.

What then? Are we to persist in sin, so that there may be all the
more grace? Once again the objector comes in, as in the parallel
place in 3.8. It is the logical sequence to Paul's thesis in 5.20,
which is precisely: the more sin the more grace. But here he
takes no more space to counter it than in chapter 3. He does not
meet it at the logical level – it cannot be so met. It is still 'No,
no!' (6.1, 15). He appeals to the facts and experience of the new
relationship in Christ – for if a man really is in that relationship
the suggestion is preposterous.

In this appeal he turns to the other half of the meaning of
faith which he has not referred to so far. Faith is not simply
complete self-emptying before *God* and his all-sufficient power
to bring new life out of a dead situation; it is faith-union with
Christ. He does not actually use the word 'faith' in the chapter

nor indeed again till his excursus in chapters 9–11. In fact there is strictly no occurrence of the characteristically Pauline theme of faith-union with Christ in the entire epistle – the greatest point of contrast with Galatians, in other ways its twin. Yet what he says about being united with Christ, being made part of the body of Christ through baptism, is the equivalent of what in other epistles he describes in terms of faith – in that 'baptism and faith are the outside and inside of the same thing' (Denney). It is worth noting, in passing, that Paul's great passages on the body of Christ and on faith do not coincide: he seldom mentions the two in the same breath. I was criticized for having mentioned faith only once in a footnote in my book *The Body* (1952). The idea is, of course, there the whole time, but I doubt if it is a sheer accident or perversion that one can write a self-consistent account of one of Paul's most central categories without mentioning the word 'faith'. It only goes to show what an extraordinarily many-sided thinker he was and how no one facet exhausts him. What is clear is that those who regard justification by faith as the only – or even, I believe, the central Pauline doctrine – are quite onesided (Albert Schweitzer in *The Mysticism of Paul the Apostle*, 1931, criticized his fellow Lutherans on this score). The argument of the epistle is, as we have seen, 'through righteousness to life', and the positive core of the letter (chapters 5–8) concerns the new being in Christ to which justification by faith is but the gate.

Verse 2. 'Dead to sin': the idea (in contrast with 'dead because of sin') is introduced as an accepted fact without warning. It is the corollary of the 'life' of which chapter 5 has spoken. The connection of thought is supplied (verse 3) by the fact and meaning of baptism as a dying with Christ. It used to be held that baptism as a dying and rising with Christ was a peculiarly Pauline doctrine, derived by him from the Hellenistic mysteries. But, quite apart from the fact that he appeals to the knowledge of it as an accepted fact with those to whom he has never preached (in both Romans and Colossians), it is now recognized (cf. R. Bultmann, *The Theology of the New Testament* I, 1952, pp. 140f.) that it goes back behind Paul to the common theology of the Hellenistic church. Indeed I am convinced that it goes back by implication to Jesus himself, who spoke of his own death as a baptism (Mark 10.38; Luke 12.50). In fact I believe that this understanding of the death of Christ as a baptism, which is the corollary of the understanding of baptism as a dying with Christ, is to be found right through the New Testament and is one of its most important ways of describing the work of Christ (cf. 'The One Baptism' in my *Twelve New Testament Studies*, 1962, pp. 158–175).

Note that baptism is 'into Christ', 'into his death' (cf. Gal. 3.27, 'as many of you were baptized into Christ put on Christ'). Baptism is essentially an act of incorporation: it brings a man into the life of the body of Christ by uniting him with his death. This is expanded in Col. 2.11–12, which runs literally: 'In whom you were circumcised with the circumcision not done by hand, in the putting off of the body of the flesh, in the circumcision of Christ, being buried with him in baptism, in which also you were raised together with him through faith in the working of God who raised him from the dead.' What baptism does is to give us a part in the death of Christ, here conceived as a circumcision, a total stripping off of the flesh of which the physical rite was the partial symbol. Through baptism Christians also, as it were, are stripped down; their body of sinful flesh is put to death and buried, and they are united with the resurrection body of Christ in which, as limbs of which, they share the new life. This is the same thought expressed a little less explicitly here in Rom. 6.1–6. The body of sin (verse 6), of the flesh (Col. 2.11), the human personality, that is, as it is controlled by sin or geared to the ends of the flesh (*not* as it is material or made of flesh), shares through baptism in the crucifying of the body of Jesus on the cross, and through it too is united with the life of his resurrection body, the corporate body of the church. This is what lies behind the pregnant words of 7.4: 'You were made dead to the law through the body of Christ, so as to be joined to another' (and the context shows that marriage–union is the analogy Paul has in mind), 'even to him who raised from the dead, that we might produce offspring for God.' There 'through the body of

69

Christ' means *both* through what Jesus did in his body on the cross *and* through the fact that you now belong to that body. You are dead to the law through your union with Christ crucified and risen, so that everything that happened to his body, both in his death and in his life, now happens in yours (cf. my book, *The Body*, chapter 2). If we ask how this critical union was effected, Paul's answer is that it is 'through baptism' (Rom. 6.4) or, more fully, 'in baptism ... through faith' (Col. 2.12). Such is the literally crucial place which baptism holds in the theology of Paul. Without baptism nothing that has been done *for* us would have any effect in our lives: for it is only here that it is done *in* us.

Verse 5. 'Incorporate with him in a death like his.' The word he uses, *symphytoi*, means united by growth, grafted into. Paul always uses organic categories in reference to the body of Christ, which he saw *primarily* as the organism of a person not as a society of people, corporeally not merely corporately (cf. again *The Body*). The phrase 'grafted into the likeness of ' is a very condensed expression and is equivalent to 'conformed to' in Rom. 8.29 and Phil. 3.21. Perhaps, to change the metaphor, we could say it means 'fused into the mould of his death'. It certainly does not imply merely an imitation of Christ, nor is there, I believe, a reference, as some have taken it, to the sacrament itself as a 'likeness' or 'miming' of his death. This, even if possible of the moment of dying, would not fit with the idea that we *shall* share the 'likeness' of his resurrection. Here Paul thinks of the resurrection mould of life as future. In Colossians it is actually *in* baptism (2.12) that we share his resurrection. There is no real contradiction: the eschatological life is always both present and future. Thus in Rom. 6.9 he says that we shall live with him; yet in 6.11 we must reckon ourselves as already 'living', and in 6.13 he refers to his converts as 'dead men raised to life'. Certainly this difference is no ground in itself for saying that Paul could not have written Colossians.

Verse 7. 'A dead man is no longer answerable for his sin'. This idea Paul will expand and illustrate in 7.1–6. It is based on the general maxim that the law has force over a man only during his life-time. Cf. the Rabbinic commonplace: 'When a man is dead he is free from the law and the commandments'. Paul's words (literally, 'he who has died he is justified from sin') *could* be taken to mean that it is death that releases a man from his sins (for this idea of being 'justified from' sins, cf. the summary of the Pauline speech in Acts 13.39). That is to say, when a man dies he automatically works off his debt because he has paid the penalty. But this would be contrary to all Paul's theology and certainly would not be justification by faith but justification by death – or even by suicide. What he must mean here is that 'the dead man has quittance from any claim that sin can make against him' (Sanday and Headlam). That is to say, when a man is dead, sin can no longer arraign him: he is out of court. By his dying with Christ the Christian is removed from the sphere of the flesh where sin has its jurisdiction, he is no longer indictable. Cf. I Peter 4.1, 'He who has suffered in the flesh (= the Pauline 'died to the flesh') has his rest from sin', he has passed outside its range.

Verse 10. 'Once and for all.' This is the great New Testament note, struck particularly by the epistle to the Hebrews (e.g., 9.26–28). Baptism is essentially unrepeatable because it represents and effects *in* the believer the once-and-for-allness of that which has been done *for* him. So Hebrews again stresses the unrepeatability of baptism (6.4). The unrepeatability of baptism is a distinctively Christian emphasis, deriving from the character of the event which it enacts within the person's life. Even if John the Baptist's baptism was unrepeated, there is no ground for thinking that this fact was regarded as its *theologically* significant difference from the 'baptisms', say, of the Essenes and others: that lay much more in the interpretation John put upon it, of deliverance from the impending judgment.

'The death that he died' or 'dying as he died': this was the unique death. All other men died 'through sin' (5.12) – their death is the sacrament and seal of sin's conquest of them. He alone died 'to' sin – he died out on it, leaving it beaten. As John Knox says (*The Death of Christ*, 1958, p. 146), the two seemingly simple expressions 'Christ died *for* sin' and 'Christ died *to*

71

sin' sum up the two ways of conceiving the death of Christ, as a sacrifice and as a victory, under which the whole of Pauline and indeed New Testament thought on the subject can be included. Here, as in Paul generally, it is the aspect of Christ's death as a victory over sin and a great liberation from sin which is dominant.

Verse 11. 'You are dead to sin: reckon yourselves to be dead to sin.' This is the first introduction of the great principle with which the rest of the chapter will be occupied, of 'become what you are'. The Christian life is always a *fait accompli* which we have to accomplish, and neither one without the other. Note also the first occurrence in Romans of the phrase 'in Christ', where it clearly has the sense of 'in union with Christ', in the body of Christ.

6.12–23

---

12 So sin must no longer reign in your mortal body, exacting obedi-
13 ence to the body's desires. You must no longer put its several
parts at sin's disposal, as implements for doing wrong. No: put
yourselves at the disposal of God, as dead men raised to life;
14 yield your bodies to him as implements for doing right; for sin
shall no longer be your master, because you are no longer under
law, but under the grace of God.

15 What then? Are we to sin, because we are not under law but
16 under grace? Of course not. You know well enough that if you
put yourselves at the disposal of a master, to obey him, you are
slaves of the master whom you obey; and this is true whether you
serve sin, with death as its result; or obedience, with righteous-
17 ness as its result. But God be thanked, you, who once were slaves
of sin, have yielded whole-hearted obedience to the pattern of
18 teaching to which you were made subject,[a] and, emancipated
19 from sin, have become slaves of righteousness (to use words that
suit your human weakness) – I mean, as you once yielded your
bodies to the service of impurity and lawlessness, making for

moral anarchy, so now you must yield them to the service of righteousness, making for a holy life.

20 When you were slaves of sin, you were free from the control of
21 righteousness; and what was the gain? Nothing but what now
22 makes you ashamed, for the end of that is death. But now, freed from the commands of sin, and bound to the service of God, your gains are such as make for holiness, and the end is eternal life.
23 For sin pays a wage, and the wage is death, but God gives freely, and his gift is eternal life, in union with Christ Jesus our Lord.

a Or which was handed on to you.

So begins the transition from the indicative to the imperative which is the point of this chapter and the answer to the false imperative of 6.1, 'Shall we persist in sin?'. 'Righteousness' in the earlier part of the epistle is primarily a matter of status revealed, bestowed; here the emphasis begins to fall on the moral content of the new life.

Verse 13. There is a subtle difference of tenses in the Greek: 'Don't go on yielding' (present) but 'dedicate yourselves once and for all' (aorist).

Verse 14. Paul returns to the indicative (though with imperatival force): 'Sin *shall* not be your master – for you are no longer under law but under grace.' Again a remark thrown out about the law which is simply laid down as a fact. This is the great new fact which is to be expounded in chapter 8 – but only after the intense conflict of chapter 7. But meanwhile the remark only gives a further handle to the objector.

Verse 15. This is another form of the objection in 6.1. Before it was: 'Shall we continue in sin in order to clock up more and more grace?' Here it is: 'Are we to sin because we are no longer under law but under grace?' The second is slightly less cynical and is indeed a typical objection to a doctrine of universalism of any kind. If God's grace is the decisive thing, does it matter what we do? All will be well in the end. Paul's scotches it, and it really is not a very profound objection to the doctrine of universally sovereign grace, though people go on putting it as if it were. If you really are under grace, living by it and not merely theorizing about it as something that will be sure to see every-one through in the end (the 'Dieu pardonnera: c'est son métier' kind of attitude), then to say that it does not matter what you do (that, as Paul puts it, you are free in regard to sin) is fantastic. Sovereign universal grace does not cut the nerve of the moral or the missionary motive, any more than it did for Paul. (For the spiritual logic of universalism I would refer to my *In the End God*, [2]1968, chapters 10 and 11.)

In this section (6.15–23) and in 7.1–6 with which it goes closely the argument is not carried any further. Paul simply adduces two analogies to bring home the truth of what he has said in 6.1–14. These analogies are 'a description of the Christian's release, what it is and what it is not' (Sanday and Head-lam). The first is from the institution of slavery, the second from that of matrimony. The first takes up the ideas of 6.12–14, the second those of 6.7–11.

Verse 16. You cannot serve sin any longer: it shall not be your boss. For, look, conversion means nothing less than change of ownership. No one can be a slave to two masters (Matt. 6.24). You can be an employee of two masters, you can do part-time work for each. But slavery as Paul's readers knew well enough – and many of them probably were or had been slaves – is total ownership. Every moment of your time is completely at the disposal of your master, there are not even working hours.

Ownership is exclusive, though the choice of master is in the first instance voluntary. Behind Paul's 'offer yourselves' 'prob-ably lies the practice whereby men applied to be taken into slavery in order to secure a livelihood' (Barrett). Sin and righte-ousness are depicted as two competing slave-owners. In verse 16b Paul, perhaps by a slip in dictation, or temporary confusion of mind, contrasts being a slave of sin – unto death – with being a slave of obedience – unto righteousness. What he must mean (for you can't intelligibly be a slave to obedience) is, as he says in verse 18, a slave of righteousness – unto life.

The idea of being a slave to sin was a commonplace: cf. John 8.34: 'Everyone who commits sin is a slave to sin'; and II Peter 2.19: 'A man is the slave of whatever has mastered him.'

74

Verse 17. Paul sees Christians having been handed over or transferred in conversion and baptism to a 'pattern of teaching' or mould of instruction. This is illuminating for Christian catechetical methods. No doubt the tradition was handed on to them, but for the purposes of his analogy of transference from one master to another Paul sees them as being handed over to the tradition and that in a set pattern of teaching. Such catechetical patterns, especially, in ethics, are clearly evidenced in the epistles. (See E. G. Selwyn's *I Peter,* 1946, pp. 363–466, and P. Carrington's *The Primitive Christian Catechism*, 1940.) He is deliberately speaking here in impersonal terms (and he admits it is only a poor analogy, verse 19), for the real relationship is not a new enslavement to anything but the freedom of sons (cf. Gal. 4.7, 'you are no longer a slave but a son', and Rom. 8.15), and in verse 22 he reverts to the personal terms of slaves to *God*, rather than to righteousness or a form of teaching, as the contrast with slaves to sin. Again at the end of the marriage analogy in 7.6 when he comes back to that of slavery he emphasizes that the new service is not to a written document but to the 'law of liberty' (James 1.25). But the analogy of slavery and indeed of the marriage-contract contains the great point he here wants to impress – that transference however voluntary does not mean that you are now free to do what you like. The closest modern parallel perhaps is not change of employment but the transfer of a football professional, often at a great price. He is not free after transfer to play for whom he likes, to shoot goals for his old team when they are playing his new one. Nor is he free under his new contract to be neutral. He has to play all out for his new club manager.

Verse 18. Paul envisages Christians as having been manumitted from slave-owner sin. The price (I Cor. 6.20; 7.23), to press the analogy, was doubtless the death of Christ, but he does not so press it as does I Peter (1.18–19), let alone ask, as Origen did, to whom was the price paid.

Verse 23. The analogy breaks down. The slave has no wages. The metaphor, if it is a live one at all, may go back to that behind the 'weapons' (*hopla*) of verse 13. The analogy is now one of mercenaries who sell their service to different commanders. The wages (*opsōnia*) are originally rations of cooked meat or fish, and so provision-money, army-pay (for the word cf. Luke 3.14: 'Soldiers ... make do with your pay'; I Cor. 9.7, 'Did you ever hear of a man serving in the army at his own expense?'). Tertullian suggests that the 'free gift' (*charisma*) may still be continuing the metaphor. He translates it by *donativum* or 'hand-out', the bonus or largesse given by the Emperor to soldiers on New Year's Day or an official birthday. But whether this is in Paul's mind or not the contrast is clear, as in that of *charisma* with *krima* in 5.16 between the process of grace and the process of law. The contrast between wages due and sheer generosity is exactly the same as that in the parable of the labourers in the vineyard in Matt. 20.1–15. There too the basis of God's action is nothing earned – as it still is in the parallel Rabbinic parable: 'This man has done more in two hours than you have in the whole day' (cf. J. Jeremias, *The Parables of Jesus*, ²1972, p. 138). It is simply, as the owner of the vineyard says, 'because I am good', or, as Paul puts it, because 'God gives freely'. Cf. earlier Rom. 4.4–5 for the same difference between what is paid as wages and counted as a gift.

7.1–6

---

7   You cannot be unaware, my friends – I am speaking to those who
     have some knowledge of law – that a person is subject to the law
2   so long as he is alive, and no longer. For example, a married
     woman is by law bound to her husband while he lives; but if her
     husband dies, she is discharged from the obligations of the
3   marriage-law. If, therefore, in her husband's lifetime she consorts with another man, she will incur the charge of adultery; but
     if her husband dies she is free of the law, and she does not
4   commit adultery by consorting with another man. So you, my
     friends, have died to the law by becoming identified with the

body of Christ, and accordingly you have found another husband in him who rose from the dead, so that we may bear fruit for
5   God. While we lived on the level of our lower nature, the sinful passions evoked by the law worked in our bodies, to bear fruit
6   for death. But now, having died to that which held us bound, we are discharged from the law, to serve God in a new way, the way of the spirit, in contrast to the old way, the way of a written code.

The general meaning is clear enough, the details the more difficult the more you inspect them – but the details of no analogy must be pressed.

The basic legal principle is that law is co-terminous with life (and this applies to law in general – both Jewish and Roman – and there is no necessary ground for assuming that Paul must be referring here to readers with a Jewish background). The normal application of this is that the law continues to have effect only so long as a man himself is alive (6.7; 7.1). But there is one case, which Paul here chooses, where the law ceases to bind a man not simply when he dies but when someone else dies – namely the marriage-contract. With the husband's death the wife is discharged from this particular section of the law. Down to the end of verse 3 the analogy is quite clear, though it is a somewhat quixotic illustration of the maxim (verse 1) that a law binds a person only so long as *he* lives. But what Paul means is obvious and the reader would probably never notice the inconsistency unless it were pointed out.

It is with verse 4 that the real difficulties of detail begin. 'You too (i.e., like the woman) were made dead (at baptism) to the law.' It seems unnecessarily perverse to suggest, with Dodd, that Paul thought of Christians as having been *married to* the law, as if the law has now become a partner to the marriage and not merely what regulated its terms. One then gets the further complication that the illustration said that the other partner died, but now it appears that the *Christian*, and not the law, has died – while in the second half of the verse he is alive to marry again. Paul, as Dodd says, may have been infelicitous in his analogies, but I cannot believe that he is really as tortuous as this. The clue surely is that 'you were made dead to the law' in verse 4 means the same as 'you were discharged from the law' in verse 6. We have been released from the power of the law because a death has taken place: it has been 'voided', or as Paul somewhat cumbrously puts it, 'we have been voided from it' or 'we have been made dead with regard to it'. No one is suggesting we have at any stage been married to it. If we ask what we were married to (who is the old husband), this is to press the analogy beyond the point at which Paul is explicit; but the implicit answer is, I believe, the flesh (*sarx*). The full exposition of the relation between the flesh, the law and sin must wait until the latter half of this chapter. But I believe that the flesh (what the NEB translates as 'our lower nature') is 'that which held us bound' (verse 6). We once lived 'in the flesh' (verse 5), the opposite of which is 'in Christ' or 'in the body of Christ'. These are the two estates of man – his former union with the flesh, his new union with Christ (verse 4), both of them thought of not merely individually but corporately, as a sphere of life in which a person has his being.

If we ask of the death that took place which party died, Paul again is not explicit. In baptism, he has said (6.3–4), Christians die, and this has probably conditioned the choice of his curious phrase 'deaded to the law', as well as the other 'voided from it'. But equally on occasion he thinks of this process not as a dying of Christians (with the implication that the flesh lives on) but as a killing off of the flesh. In 8.13 he speaks of Christians continuing what was begun at baptism in terms of putting to death the 'deeds of the body' (here equivalent to the flesh) and in Col. 3.5 of mortifying 'your earthly members', i.e., again, the flesh with its passions. Yet Paul constantly veers from one idea to the other, for he has just said in Col. 3.3, 'you died and your life has been hidden with Christ in God'. The truth is that the 'body of flesh' which is killed off is in fact not anything so remote even as the other partner in a marriage, but the very self or ego, the personality as it is organized for sin. Therefore to say 'you kill it off' is the equivalent of saying 'you are killed'.

The marriage analogy breaks down. Yet it takes Paul a long

way. For we must remember that for the Hebrew the marriage–union makes literally 'one flesh' or one body, and Christians are that with Christ (Eph. 5.28–32). The two unions are absolutely exclusive (I Cor. 6.13–20). Being one body with Christ is possible only if Christians have been utterly severed from their former union with the flesh. To go back on that is to destroy the very possibility of being *in* Christ. Hence Paul's vehemence in Galatians against those who by receiving circumcision wed themselves again to the flesh and the law: 'You are severed from Christ, you who would be justified by the law' (Gal. 5.4). This exclusive claim is the same lesson which the analogy from slave-ownership pressed home; and this is the real value of both examples, which is not destroyed by any incoherence of detail.

Now in the second analogy he has silently slipped from sin to the law as that which stands as the opposite of union with Christ. Moreover in the course of 7.1–6 the word *nomos* shifts its meaning in a most slippery way. It starts off (verse 1) as law in general – as we might say 'in law'. It then becomes (verse 2b) a specific piece of legislation 'the law of the husband', i.e. the marriage–statute, which is subsequently (verse 3) referred to simply as 'the law'. From there the transition is made to 'the law', unspecified, from which Christians are released by the death which has occurred (verse 4). By verse 5 it is clear that Paul has identified this with the Jewish Torah, *the* law, on which subject again he hangs out his bat in a way that he seems to find irresistible. He makes the unargued statement that it is through the instrumentality of the law that the passions of sin ravage our bodies and produce death. And it is in fact this underlying, but unstated, assumption, that sin is in some way a function of law, that allows him silently to equate the effects of law and sin and to pass from the one to the other in parallel analogies. Finally (verse 6), the law is identified with a written code, or *gramma*, which is set in complete contrast with the way of the Spirit of God.

'What then are we to say?', he goes on in verse 7. 'Is the law identical with sin?' It would indeed begin to look like it. By now he can postpone a thorough reckoning with the law and its status no longer.

But first it is worth recapitulating what Paul has thrown out on the subject of the law so far, so that we can see how he takes it all up in 7.7–8.4:

3.20: 'No human being can be justified in the sight of God for having kept the law: law brings only the consciousness of sin.'

3.31: 'Does this mean that we are using faith to undermine law? By no means: we are placing law itself on a firmer footing.'

4.15: 'Law can bring only retribution; but where there is no law there can be no breach of the law.'

5.13: 'Sin was already in the world before there was law, though in the absence of law no reckoning was kept of sin.'

5.20: 'Law intruded into this process to multiply law-breaking.'

6.14: 'You are no longer under law, but under the grace of God.'

7.5: 'While we lived on the level of our lower nature, the sinful passions evoked by the law worked in our bodies, to bear fruit for death.'

7.6: 'We are discharged from the law, to serve God in a new way, the way of the spirit, in contrast to the old way, the way of a written code.'

All this can be summed up as saying: The law is quite useless for putting a man right with God, it merely brings guilt and deepens sin. It evokes and provokes the passions, and its effect is nothing but retribution and finally death. It is the opposite of being under the grace of God and it is the opposite to the Spirit of God. No wonder the question arises, 'Is the law identical with sin?', and no wonder that some justification is due of the remark that all Paul is doing is to place law on a firmer footing! To both he addresses himself in what follows.

7   What follows? Is the law identical with sin? Of course not. But except through law I should never have become acquainted with sin. For example, I should never have known what it was to

8   covet, if the law had not said, 'Thou shalt not covet.' Through that commandment sin found its opportunity, and produced in me all kinds of wrong desires. In the absence of law, sin is a dead

9   thing. There was a time when, in the absence of law, I was fully alive; but when the commandment came, sin sprang to life and I

10 died. The commandment which should have led to life proved in

11 my experience to lead to death, because sin found its opportunity in the commandment, seduced me, and through the command-ment killed me.

12 Therefore the law is in itself holy, and the commandment is

13 holy and just and good. Are we to say then that this good thing was the death of me? By no means. It was sin that killed me, and thereby sin exposed its true character: it used a good thing to bring about my death, and so, through the commandment, sin became more sinful than ever.

14 We know that the law is spiritual; but I am not: I am

15 unspiritual, the purchased slave of sin. I do not even acknow-ledge my own actions as mine, for what I do is not what I want to

16 do, but what I detest. But if what I do is against my will, it means

17 that I agree with the law and hold it to be admirable. But as things are, it is no longer I who perform the action, but sin that

18 lodges in me. For I know that nothing good lodges in me – in my unspiritual nature, I mean – for though the will to do good is

19 there, the deed is not. The good which I want to do, I fail to do;

20 but what I do is the wrong which is against my will; and if what I do is against my will, clearly it is no longer I who am the agent, but sin that has its lodging in me.

21 I discover this principle, then: that when I want to do the right,

22 only the wrong is within my reach. In my inmost self I delight in

23 the law of God, but I perceive that there is in my bodily members a different law, fighting against the law that my reason approves and making me a prisoner under the law^a that is in my members,

24 the law of sin. Miserable creature that I am, who is there to rescue me out of this body doomed to death^b? God alone,

81

25   through Jesus Christ our Lord! Thanks be to God! In a word
      then, I myself, subject to God's law as a rational being, am yet,[c]
      in my unspiritual nature, a slave to the law of sin.

8   The conclusion of the matter is this: there is no condemnation
2   for those who are united with Christ Jesus, because in Christ
      Jesus the life-giving law of the Spirit has set you free from the
3   law of sin and death. What the law could never do, because our
      lower nature robbed it of all potency, God has done: by sending
      his own Son in a form like that of our own sinful nature, and as a
      sacrifice for sin,[d] he has passed judgement against sin within that
4   very nature, so that the commandment of the law may find
      fulfilment in us, whose conduct, no longer under the control of
      our lower nature, is directed by the Spirit.

a   *Or* by means of the law.
b   *Or* out of the body doomed to this death.
c   *Or* Thus, left to myself, while subject ... rational being, I am yet....
d   *Or* and to deal with sin.

More ink, I suppose, has been spilled over this passage of
Romans than any other. Quite apart from the details of
exegesis, which are not all that difficult, two questions have
agitated interpreters: (*a*) Does the use of the first person singu-
lar indicate genuine autobiography – or is it simply cast in the
first person for vividness? and (*b*) Does it refer to the Christian
or to the pre-Christian state – is the use of the present from
verse 14 onwards again merely for vividness?

To (*a*) there is fairly general, though by no means universal,
agreement that it is a genuine summing up of Paul's actual
experience, and the conclusion (verses 24–25) is too heartfelt to
be a purely ideal reconstruction in which 'one' could be substi-
tuted for 'I' without loss. Paul is drawing on personal experience; yet it is dangerous to use it simply as autobiography, for
clearly he is talking generally of the condition described as typical of man under the law.

(*b*) is much more difficult to decide. For a full and excellent
discussion, see C. L. Mitton, 'Romans vii Reconsidered', *The
Expository Times*, 65, 1953–4, pp. 78–81, 99–103, 132–5. His
eventual conclusion is not unlike mine, though not entirely the

same. One thing is certain, and that is that 'no one could have written the passage but a Christian' (Denney). Even if the whole represents Paul looking back on his pre-Christian state (and verses 7–13 are clearly set in the past and refer presumably to Paul's youth), then it is his pre-Christian state seen through Christian eyes. It is highly doubtful if it can be read as a transcript of 'Paul's own state when he set out for Damascus' (Dodd). There is no evidence that *at that time* he did feel a broken man in regard to the law. Whatever his unconscious turmoil – and Acts suggests that this was caused by the witness of *Christians*, like Stephen, and his inability any longer to kick against the pricks, rather than by having reached the end of his tether as a Jew – it is clear that Paul himself in describing his own conversion never sees it like this. His description in Phil. 3.4–7 of his state as a Jewish Pharisee reads very differently: 'A Hebrew born and bred; in my attitude to the law, a Pharisee; in pious zeal, a persecutor of the church; in legal rectitude, faultless.' All these he regards as valuable assets he was prepared to write off, not as a way of life which was by then paying no dividends anyhow. These assets were indeed grounds for real confidence. If Paul came to such an analysis of the effects of the law and of his pre-Christian condition as he gives in Rom. 7 it is certainly a post-Christian analysis. So much is, or should be, agreed, and it is particularly emphasized by such different writers as Denney and Bultmann.

But this still leaves us with the question, what is Paul purporting to describe – his past life or his present – however postconversion his description of it? The division of interpreters goes right back. As a description of:

(*a*) *unregenerate or pre-Christian man*: Origen and the mass of the Greek Fathers, German Pietism, Wesley, and the majority of modern commentators and translators – e.g. Sanday and Headlam, Denney (with qualifications), Gore, Kirk, Moffatt, Dodd, J. B. Phillips, Bultmann and Kümmel (in his *Introduction to the New Testament*, ET, ²1975).

(*b*) *regenerate or Christian man*: Augustine and the Latin Fathers generally, Luther, Calvin, Barth, Nygren and Cranfield.

Leenhardt makes the interesting point that those who support this side tend to be dogmaticians rather than exegetes. Cranfield is an exception, but a Calvinist. (Cranfield claims Barrett, but he is not really on either side.)

Barth describes Paul as misunderstood by those modern theologians who read him through the spectacles of their own piety. But the line-up suggests that both sides may be wearing spectacles and that in each case the judgment is made as much for subjective theological reasons as by any objective canon of exegesis. The question ultimately comes down to: *Could* Paul have said this or that as a Christian? And the answer will largely depend on one's experience of what being a Christian means. It is no good only looking at Paul: one must look within. The Arminian finds one thing, the Calvinist another – and who is to say which understands Paul the better?

But there are certain objective factors to be considered – though it is hardly to be expected from the division that they will all point one way.

(*a*) The arguments for the view that the whole chapter relates to Paul's past history, before he became a Christian.

1. *Within the passage itself.* There is the contrast between chapters 7 and 8. The two cannot be descriptions of the same life. There is no single expression in chapter 7 (till the parenthesis of verse 25) which is distinctively Christian – no mention of Christ or the Spirit. The contrast in chapter 8 is glaring: it is the very character of Christian liberation.

2. *Within the epistle as a whole.* In 6.20–22 the transition from the old life is described as over: 'When you were slaves of sin, you were free from the control of righteousness; and what was the gain? Nothing but what now makes you ashamed, for the end of that is death. But now, freed from the commands of sin, and bound to the service of God, your gains are such as to make for holiness, and the end is eternal life.' If Paul means anything there by the aorist 'freed from the commands of sin', how can he describe himself as at this moment 'sin's purchased slave' (7.14), the very thing he no longer is in chapter 6, and a 'wretched man' still needing deliverance (7.24)?

3. *Within Paul's writings as a whole*. Nowhere else does Paul speak thus of the present Christian life, which is always depicted in terms of peace, joy and victory, even as he admits that he is the chief of sinners.

(*b*) The arguments for the view that Paul is speaking of present Christian existence.

1. *Within the passage*. Verses 7–13 are in the past tense; 14–25 in the present. Why this transition if it is not significant? Nygren argues that this corresponds to the division in 7.5–6 between the pre-Christian and the Christian life: 'While we lived on the level of our lower nature, the sinful passions evoked by the law worked in our bodies, to yield fruit for death. But now, having died to that which held us bound, we are discharged from the law to serve God in a new way.' Verses 7–13 describe what the Christian was before. In that situation the law was a power – but only to provoke and increase sin: it was a power for death. Verses 14–25 on the other hand describe what the Christian is now. One would expect perhaps that the law would now be the power for good which previously it was for evil. But no. True, it cannot now bring death – but neither can it bring life. It is strictly power*less*. But (8.3) what the law was impotent to do, God has done. In verses 7–13 and 14–25 Paul is describing the two situations (pre-Christian and Christian) *both from the point of view of the law*. And from that point of view there is not much positive difference. Even for the redeemed life the law has no positive value. It is powerless to do any more *to* us, but it is equally powerless to do any more *for* us. Hence the generally depressing tone of the chapter, which is relieved only when the same situation is seen *from the point of view of the Spirit of God*. Verses 14–25 describe the Christian life, but the Christian life, not from the point of view of its quickening power, but, as it were, from the point of view of a nerve that has been cut.

2. *Within the epistle*. Chapters 5–8 all describe the Christian life: 5 deliverance from wrath, 6 from sin, 7 from the law, 8 from death. Reversion to non-Christian existence would destroy the whole sequence. The theme of chapter 7 is our deliver-

ance from the law, with the corollary stated of its impotence to deliver us.

3. *Within Paul's writings.* Description of conflict even within the Christian life is not inconsistent with Paul elsewhere. Thus we have in Rom. 8.23: 'Even we to whom the Spirit is given ... are groaning inwardly while we wait for God to make us his sons and set our whole body free'; and especialiy in Gal. 5.17: 'The lower nature sets its desires against the Spirit, while the Spirit fights against it. They are in conflict with one another so that what you will to do you cannot do.' Nygren stresses the fact that in Rom. 7 man's *will* is wholly for the good: it is not in itself divided or evil. If this is a description of man outside Christ it does not tally with the description of the non-Christian he gave in 1.18–3.20. Nor, as we have seen, does Rom. 7 fit with Paul's own complete self-satisfaction as a Pharisee in Phil. 3.6. What Rom. 7 describes, says Nygren, is the position of the Christian – yet the Christian who is still living within this age, in the flesh, which prevents him achieving what he wants to do. Indeed, he says that if a Christian could ever get beyond the position of Rom. 7 (which is *not* one of despair but of thanks and victory through Jesus Christ) and claim even as a Christian to fulfil the law, then the law would once again become a way of salvation. No, the Christian is free of the righteousness of the law altogether. The righteousness of God has nothing to do with success *even as a Christian* in keeping the law.

Both positions in fact are open to serious weaknesses.

1. *In the passage itself* there is in verse 14 a transition to the present which the first view (that it is all about the past) ignores. Yet the transition is so unobtrusive that it is difficult to put the weight on it that Nygren claims. There is no such clear contrast between 'then' and 'now' as between 7.5 and 7.6.

2. *In relation to the rest of the epistle* one cannot say with Nygren that the whole of chapters 5–8 are concerned with the Christian life. 7.7–13 confessedly are not – then why not verses 14–25? Yet, on the other side, it is certainly not made plain by Paul that verses 14–25 refer to the past, as it is unequivocally elsewhere when he is talking about 'the life we once lived'.

Moreover, if verses 14–25 are a description of a past state on which Paul can now look back as something from which, thank God, he has been delivered, then the climax and conclusion of the chapter should be verses 24–25a: 'Miserable creature that I am, who is there to rescue me out of this body doomed to death? God alone, through Jesus Christ our Lord! Thanks be to God!' – leading straight into the triumphant sequel of chapter 8. To put *after* this, as a summary of the chapter, verse 25b, 'In a word then, I myself, subject to God's law as a rational being, am yet, in my unspiritual nature, a slave to the law of sin', is an intolerable inversion and bathos. It suggests that he is not out of the wood after all. So we find Moffatt (supported by Dodd and Phillips and Black) transposing the verse-order and placing 25b before 24–25a. They may be right, but there is not the slightest manuscript evidence for it; and it is certainly a weakness in any argument that finds this necessary. Nygren is here on strong ground.

3. *In comparison with the rest of Paul* Nygren is *not* entirely happy. True there are parallels, but the tone even of the most groaning passages in Rom. 8 *is* different from the *cri de coeur* of the wretch sold under sin in Rom. 7. Moreover, Nygren's triumphant quotation of Gal. 5.17 ignores the previous verse 5.16: 'If you are guided by the Spirit you will *not* fulfil the desires of your lower nature.' There is a promise of real mystery for the Christian. Nor is it convincing to say with Nygren that Rom. 7 cannot describe the non-Christian, because such a man cannot be said to approve the law of God with an undivided mind. For in chapters 1 and 2 Paul has made the point that the Gentile *does* know God and his natural reason *does* tell him what is good; even more so is this true of the Jew who approves the law and knows God's will (2.17–18) precisely as 7.16 and 22 depict – but is yet unable or unwilling to practise it. Again Nygren's argument that the agonising tone of verses 14–25 cannot refer to Paul's pre-Christian life because in Philippians Paul describes his state of mind as Pharisee so differently is not decisive against both passages referring to the same period. Paul in Philippians is boasting of the *outward* assets he could show, and

external rectitude is quite compatible with a knowledge of real inner failure. Mitton cites Luther: 'However irreproachable my life as a monk, I felt myself, in the presence of God, to be a sinner with a most unquiet conscience' (1519); and 'I was a good monk and kept strictly to my order.... All my companions who knew me would bear witness to that' (1533). Lastly, to say with Nygren that the Christian has no right to claim real moral achievement, that the righteousness required by the law has nothing to do with the righteousness of faith, ignores Paul's conclusion in 8.3–4, where he specifically says that Christ has done what the law could not do, 'so that the commandment of the law may find fulfilment in us, whose conduct, no longer under the control of our lower nature, is directed by the Spirit'. To claim that is *not* to slip back into salvation by law: it is to press forward to Christian perfection.

One can really say that neither position has established itself against the other. 'Obviously the problem is a little too complicated to be solved by a single Yes or No' (Brunner). It begins to look as if both theses – that it represents wholly pre-Christian experience or wholly Christian experience – may result from asking the wrong question. I believe that the concentration on the *time*-reference (past or present) has put people on the wrong track, so that the real clue has been missed. The transition from past to present in verses 13–14 is in fact quite unmarked; and any view which seizes on this as the clue has I believe not only grabbed the wrong one but thereby misses the real one, which is in fact planted at this very turn in the argument.

If we ask why the present is introduced at all, it is to express the purely general proposition that 'the law is spiritual'. That is followed by the contrast: 'but I am fleshly'. The contrast is not, with Nygren, between what I was and I am. The time-reference in 'am' is entirely unimportant. It is a general timeless proposition, like the previous one. The contrast, and it is a strong one, is not between what I was and am, but between the law and myself (the *ego* in the Greek is emphatic). The law is all right, in fact it is divine; but human nature is incapable of fulfilling it.

The contrast is between the law, representing the will of God, which belongs to the sphere of spirit, and mere human nature left to itself, man in his distance and difference from God and all that is spirit, that is man as flesh (*sarx*). When Paul uses the word *ego* here he has not in mind either Paul the Jew or Paul the Christian but Paul simply *qua* man, the self in its own unaided human nature, or in biblical terms, man as 'flesh' (*sarx*). The *ego*, he says, is *sarkinos*. Now Paul is pretty consistent in his use of the distinction between the two Greek words *sarkinos* and *sarkikos*. *Sarkinos* literally means made of flesh (e.g.,of tablets in II Cor. 3.3). The *locus classicus* for the distinction is I Cor. 3.1–3: 'Previously I was not able to speak to you as "spiritual" (i.e. as the mature, advanced Christians you claim to be) but as *sarkinoi*. I had to treat you as you treat babies, as though they were just flesh. I had to feed you on slops not meat, for you could not take anything else. But even now you still cannot take anything different. You are still "fleshly"; but now the trouble is different. You are *sarkikoi* – that is, you are living *by* the flesh, as if the *sarx* and its ends were the sole norm of conduct. For seeing there is jealousy and schism among you (not babies' sins) does not that show that you are *sarkikoi*, living simply by the standards and in the power of unregenerate human nature? How can I talk to you as spiritual?' *Sarkinos* is the equivalent of being 'in the flesh' (*en sarki*), being mere flesh. *Sarkikos* is the equivalent of living 'according to the flesh' (*kata sarka*), with the outlook of the flesh (Rom. 8.5).

Here in 7.14 Paul uses *sarkinos*. He is talking quite neutrally about the state of human nature in its own strength. It belongs to the realm of flesh – and the realm of flesh is occupied territory, it is enslaved, sold over to sin. This is just a fact, as Paul sees it. He is not saying that as a Christian he is in hopeless bondage or that as a Jew he was; but simply that *qua* flesh he is in sin's jurisdiction and domain, just as in 8.3 he says that Christ took flesh that belonged to sin. *Sarkinos* is not a morally derogatory term, as 'carnal' (AV and RSV) suggest to us, but a neutral fact. The law is spiritual, but I am flesh – and as such sin's tributary.

Paul then proceeds to describe man's helplessness *qua sarx* or flesh. That this is what 'I' here means is confirmed by verse 18, where 'in me' is explained and defined as 'that is, in my flesh'. I have tried to show in *The Body* (chapter 1) that *sarx* is characteristically used, like the other parts of the body in biblical language, not to set one part of man in contrast with another part, so much as to describe the whole of man viewed under one aspect in contrast with the whole of man viewed under another. *Sarx* (flesh) equals man as *sarx*, *sōma* (body) equals man as *sōma*, etc. Man *qua sarx* is man viewed in his difference and distance from God, man left to his own weakness and mortality. So here the explanatory phrase 'that is, in my flesh' does not mean in that part of me which is flesh, so that the *ego* itself is something other than flesh (and therefore not sinful), but 'in me, that is in my own unaided human nature'. By himself, man in his own strength is impotent to do good. For the *ego* has lost control of its own actions: 'I do not choose what I do' (verse 15). Yet, Paul insists, human nature, man as *sarx*, is by no means simply evil. He has become a battlefield in which he is divided against himself. There is a resistance movement which desires something quite different from this occupation by sin; but there is also a collaborationist element which becomes the willing tool of sin. On the one hand, the *ego*, the very *ego* which is *sarkinos* (verse 14), agrees with the law of God (verse 16). But the *ego* also agrees (because it is *sarkikos*) with the law of sin. And so complete is the bondage in which this agreement has got man that it can be said simply that *qua* flesh I am its willing slave (verse 25).

The result is a pathetic and an abject state – like that of any occupied country which would prefer not to be collaborationist but cannot help itself. But it is important to notice what it is that is wretched or miserable (verse 24). It is not Paul as a Jew (what he once was), nor Paul as a Christian (what he is now in Christ), but Paul as a mere man (*ego anthrōpos*), facing the law by himself, in his own resources: 'Miserable creature that I am, who is there to deliver me from this solidarity in death to which the flesh is subject? God alone, through Jesus Christ our Lord!'

Here Paul does indeed speak as a Christian, knowing that man is *not* in fact left to himself – he is not mere flesh. Indeed his *presuppositions* have been Christian throughout, though for the purposes of his estimate of the law he has been confronting it not with man in Christ but with human nature in its own strength, the natural Adam (and the *anthrōpos* of verse 24 may well take up in Greek form the implicit allusion to Adam in verse 11). For it is this humanity that the law has to work on and work through. This is therefore the relevant analysis when assessing the power of the law to achieve its end. And of this analysis the conclusion is not the ejaculation of verse 25, which is here thrown in only to anticipate the argument of 8.1–4. It is, quite rightly and in its proper place, verse 25b. For of this encounter between the law and mere human nature, what is the outcome? It is, says Paul, that *autos ego*, which is not just 'I myself', which would be *ego*, but I 'left to myself' (NEB margin), I 'on my own' (Good News Bible), am in a hopelessly divided state. His point is that the law, however good and spiritual, is impotent to overcome this division: for 'our lower nature robbed it of all potency' (8.3). Only Christ can overcome the conflict, because he deals with sin in a way that the law could not (8.3). The purpose of the argument in 7.7–25 is not (as Nygren says) to show how the Christian is freed from the law (that is the purpose of 8.1–4, though the answer is fore-shadowed in the interjection of verse 25a), but to show why, *although* the law is 'spiritual' (and therefore *not* identical with sin 7.7)), it can do nothing for man who is 'fleshly' (and there-fore identified with sin).

Chapter 7 is really not adding anything to the previous argu-ment, so much as justifying in one sustained piece of analysis his various *obiter dicta* on the law.

In the light of this then let us try and sum up what Paul says about the law, picking up particularly what we have left untreated in 7.7–13.

'Is the law identical with sin?' We have seen reason to realize that this question has become very pressing – as all that he has said so far appears to have pointed in this direction. Heaven forbid! *But* the fact remains that 'except through law I should never have become acquainted with sin' (7.7). Paul certainly does not mean that he wasn't a sinner before he became conscious of the law – sin (*hamartia*) precedes the law (5.13). But he would not have come to know sin for what it really was. And this is what he said in his first remark about the law back in 3.20: 'Through law comes the recognition or consciousness of sin.' It was the law saying 'Thou shalt not covet' that really brought home what coveting meant.

But now he goes on, without explicitly stating the fact, to say something further, to which he has also alluded darkly before. The law not only makes law-breaking (*parabasis*) possible (4.15); it came in actually to 'multiply law-breaking' (5.20), to increase it in extent as well as in guilt. For when law is absent sin is dormant (7.8). In this situation the self, as Paul remembers, did have a real life and vitality of its own (7.9). But then the law comes along, and the original innocence is lost.

Now human nature or 'flesh', it cannot be overstressed, is not for Paul or for biblical thought in itself *evil*. But it *is* weak and mortal – it is the antithesis of God who is 'spirit', power (cf. the *locus classicus* in Isa. 31.3: 'The Egyptians are men, and not God; and their horses flesh, not spirit', i.e., they are weak, not invincible). The flesh is weak territory, lying exposed to any attack that comes along. Now in this territory sin has secured a foothold, a bridge-head, a base of operations (7.8). How did it do it? It did it 'through the commandment', which it employed as a sort of Trojan horse. It got in under cover of this good thing (7.13) and deceived the old Adam, who was entirely gullible (7.11). Sin 'beguiled' me as the serpent 'beguiled' Eve (cf. II Cor. 11.3). The law then, which was good and intended to promote life (7.10–13), was used as the tool of sin and became an instrument for death. Paul sums up the process in I Cor. 15.56: 'The sting of death is sin' (not as we use the phrase to mean the real gravamen, but literally that through which death makes its jab and effects its entry into the human situation – cf. Rom. 5.12: 'through sin death'); 'and the power of sin is the law' (i.e., that through which sin 'comes to power', enters upon its reign or mastery (6.12, 14)). And the baleful sequence of the law leading to sin and resulting in death, which he describes in 7.11, 'Sin found its opportunity in the commandment, seduced me, and through the commandment killed me', only repeats what he had outlined previously in 7.5: 'The sinful passions evoked by the law worked in our bodies, to bear fruit for death.' And, as the opening of that verse makes clear, the whole process was possible because we were 'in the flesh'. For the flesh is 'that which held us bound' (7.6), the seat and ground of this entire servitude. So it is that Paul is forced to go on, as we have seen, to an analysis of man as 'flesh'. For therein lies the whole problem, that while the law is indeed 'spiritual' and of God, its only effect is death. It 'works' death (7.13), which is the end-term of his earlier statement that it simply 'works' wrath (4.15). All it does is to make sin 'more sinful than ever' (7.13).

Paul has now taken up and justified all his remarks about the law except three: 3.31: 'Does this mean that we are using faith to undermine law? By no means: we are placing law itself on a firmer footing'; 6.14: 'You are no longer under law, but under the grace of God'; and 7.6: 'We are discharged from the law to serve God in a new way, the way of the spirit, in contrast to the old way, the way of a written code.' These three propositions he now substantiates in 8.1–4.

Verse 1. The contrast is between man in himself and man in Christ, between the 'I on my own' of 7.25 and the 'you are not your own' of I Cor. 6.19.

Verse 2 justifies the earlier statement that we are no longer under the power of law but under grace. The slavery *has* been broken to 'the law of sin and death', which means probably *both* the principle or rule of sin and death (in contrast with the rule of the Spirit in verse 2a) *and* the law (the Torah) which leads to sin and death (as in chapter 7 and clearly in verse 3a). This is a typical Pauline transition, with one use of *nomos* sliding into another.

Verse 3. The law for all the fact that it is 'spiritual' could not give life. It is a written code that kills. Indeed it has actually to be opposed by the Spirit, not again by 'the spirit of the law' as

93

opposed to 'the letter of the law', but by the life-giving Spirit of God, itself seen as a ruling principle or norm (*nomos*). That the law cannot itself give life is Paul's real charge against it. In Gal. 3.21 he goes so far as to say, 'If a law had been given which had power to bestow life, then indeed righteousness would have come from keeping the law'. Well, here is a law which *does* give life, the *nomos* of the Spirit of life in Christ Jesus. Yet fundamentally it is not a law at all: it is an act of God. What is the difference?

The law was impotent because it could only be as strong as the flesh through which it had to be implemented, and the flesh was hopelessly under the power of sin. But then God intervened. He actually sent his Son to share and to bear this flesh *which belonged to sin*. On this complete identification of Christ even with fallen human nature, see again *The Body*, chapter 2, where the position I take is supported both by Barth and Barrett. But he did it also to deal with sin, 'as a sacrifice for sin'. The phrase *'peri hamartias'* may well have this overtone: cf. Lev. 4, of the sin-offering, and Heb. 10.6, 26. Yet the sacrificial imagery if present is not explicit. Paul draws out the meaning rather in his preferred categories of the law-courts: 'He condemned sin in the flesh.' It is the same juridical metaphor that he used in 6.7: 'The dead man has his quittance from anything that sin can bring against him.' Sin is regarded as the prosecution, man as the defendant, in God's court. Anyone who is 'in the flesh' comes within the province of sin. Sin puts in its regular claim against him, requesting the sentence of death which is the 'end' of sin. In every other human instance sin has won its case – the death penalty has been granted universally (cf. 5.12). But now Jesus, the Judge's own son, appears 'in the flesh'. Sin stakes its usual claim for him. But he has given sin no handle or foothold, and in this unique case it is the defendant who is acquitted and sin who is condemned. Or, put positively, 'he (Christ) condemned sin' – and that 'in the flesh', within the very human nature by identification with which he became exposed to sin at all. The incarnation is the essential prerequisite of the atonement for Paul. (There is no contrast here between Paul and

John.) Cf. Col. 1.22: 'he reconciled (you) in the body of his flesh through death'. But the body of his flesh, what he did in the incarnation and cross, does not stand alone as a unique exception in the case-history of sin, so that after him everything goes on the same. His victory is shared by those who now belong to that body. (The church as well as the incarnation is an indispensable part of Paul's doctrine of the atonement.) Those who are 'in Christ Jesus', in the body of Christ, are equally free from condemnation (verse 1). And the purpose of it all is precisely that the *dikaiōma* of the law, what the law defines as 'righteous', may find fulfilment in us (verse 4), who, though at one level still 'in the flesh', are now empowered to live no longer 'according to the flesh', with lives determined simply by its norms and destiny, but 'according to the spirit', controlled by the supernatural life of God.

So by the end of verse 4 Paul has taken up and justified his three remaining theses about the law: (*a*) that 'we are now no longer under the regime of law but of grace' (6.14); (*b*) that this is a regimen of spirit, which has superseded the killing regimen of 'the letter' (7.6); and (*c*), most improbably, that he *is* establishing the law (3.31); for not only can this regimen be described in a real sense as a *nomos*, the true divine norm of life, but it actually fulfils rather than abolishes the Mosaic law. For, in the life and power of the Spirit, Christians can really live up to it. He will return to this in 13.8–10, where he says that the man who loves his neighbour in Christ has satisfied every claim of the law, and in 10.4, where Christ is described as 'the end of the law unto righteousness for all who believe', which probably means *both* the end of the law as a way to get right with God *and* the fulfilment of the law in such a way that a real righteousness does result for all who believe.

Thus Paul, having worked his way through the jungle of sin, law and death, is now poised to expatiate on the glorious freedom of the new life in Christ.

5 Those who live on the level of our lower nature have their out-
6 look formed by it, and that spells death; but those who live on
the level of the spirit have the spiritual outlook, and that is life
7 and peace. For the outlook of the lower nature is enmity with
God; it is not subject to the law of God; indeed it cannot be:
8 those who live on such a level cannot possibly please God.
9   But that is not how you live. You are on the spiritual level, if
only God's Spirit dwells within you; and if a man does not pos-
10 sess the Spirit of Christ, he is no Christian. But if Christ is dwelling within you, then although the body is a dead thing because
you sinned, yet the spirit is life itself because you have been
11 justified.*a* Moreover, if the Spirit of him who raised Jesus from
the dead dwells within you, then the God who raised Christ Jesus
from the dead will also give new life to your mortal bodies
through his indwelling Spirit.
12   It follows, my friends, that our lower nature has no claim upon
us; we are not obliged to live on that level. If you do so, you must
13 die. But if by the Spirit you put to death all the base pursuits of
the body, then you will live.

a Or so that you may live rightly.

Paul has just introduced (verse 4) for the first time in the epistle
the phrase 'according to the flesh' (*kata sarka*) and he here
elaborates its meaning. He is not consistent in distinguishing it
from 'in the flesh' (*en sarki*) – or rather he uses *en sarki* in an
equivocal sense. In II Cor. 10.3 he does contrast the two quite
clearly: 'Though we walk in the flesh, we do not war according
to the flesh.' To be in the flesh is simply a description of being in
this world – it is man's natural God-given sphere (cf. Gal. 2.20;
Phil. 1.24; etc.). Yet to be *en sarki* is *ipso facto* to be in the flesh
which belongs to sin – and he can contrast it with being 'in
Christ' or 'in the Spirit' as man's redeemed sphere of life: cf.
Rom. 7.5, 'when we *were* in the flesh'; 8.9, 'but you are not in
the flesh'. 'In the flesh' here means within the sphere and there-

fore the jurisdiction of the world and its forces, and in this sense 'those that are in the flesh cannot please God' (verse 8).

But this is what Paul more usually expresses by living 'according to the flesh' (verse 5). *Kata sarka* too can be used in a purely neutral sense of natural descent – e.g., 1.3, 'born of the seed of David according to the flesh'; 4.1, 'Abraham our forefather according to the flesh'. Yet what is *kata sarka* is very often the antithesis of what is *kata pneuma*, 'according to the spirit' (e.g., Gal. 4.29); and Israel 'after the flesh' (I Cor. 10.18) is distinguished from the Christian church, the true Israel of God. To live *kata sarka* is to accept the fact of the flesh as one's sole horizon and criterion. It is to allow one's 'being in the world' to determine one's whole outlook. Living 'according to the flesh' or 'the outlook of the flesh' is the nearest equivalent to 'materialism', though it is quite misleading to identify 'the flesh' *tout court* with matter, as it includes what we should call the things of the mind, and most of the sins of the flesh are far from merely sensual (Gal. 5.19–21). This outlook of the flesh is 'death' because it accepts the end of the flesh as the end of everything – and the end of the flesh is corruption (verse 13). To accept the flesh as one's end is to regard it as an end in itself rather than subjecting it to the law of God. Therefore to live 'according to the flesh' is *ipso facto* not to be subject to the law of God (verse 7). It is to erect the flesh itself into an idol: compare Phil. 3.19, 'whose God is their belly', and Rom. 16.17–18, where those who 'serve their own belly' are not gluttons but those who 'cause divisions and occasions of stumbling' (it is the equivalent of being *sarkikos* in I Cor. 3.3). Hence 'the outlook of the flesh' is by definition 'enmity with God'.

In verses 8–9 there is a transition to the contrast between 'in the flesh' and 'in the spirit'. Your native sphere of life is not in the flesh, so that your horizon should be determined by it. You are in the sphere of the spirit, 'if God's Spirit dwells within you'. Then there is the further transition from 'the Spirit of God' to 'the Spirit of Christ' and from being 'of Christ' to 'Christ being in you'. There is no distinction in experience between these realities of the new life. But this does not mean that Paul

97

identifies the Spirit with Christ any more than he identifies Christ with the Father, though he can predicate the same functions and effects of each. (It is often said that he does quite specifically identify Christ and the Spirit in one place, i.e., in II Cor. 3.17: 'the Lord is the Spirit'. But I am certain that this is not what he means and that the NEB is right in referring 'the Lord' here to the God of the Old Testament: 'Now the Lord of whom this passage speaks is the Spirit.')

Verses 10–11. Paul now says the same thing in terms of *sōma*, body. Again I must refer to the discussion of this in *The Body*, especially pp. 26–33. It is enough here to say that though *sōma*, body, is frequently identified with *sarx*, flesh, it is not identical with it. The end of man as *sarx* is corruption, but man as *sōma* is 'for the Lord' (I Cor. 6.13). But in sinful man the body is completely subjected to the ends of the *sarx* and can therefore virtually be equated with it. It is a 'body of sin' (Rom. 6.6) just as the flesh is the 'flesh of sin' (8.3). It shares the mortality of the *sarx*: it is a 'mortal body' (6.12), which is not merely a natural mortality but 'the body of this death' (7.24); it is doomed to the fate of 'the flesh'. So here in verse 10 the body is a dead thing because of sin. The deeds of the body have to be put to death (verse 13), and these represent the whole way of life 'according to the flesh'. The two seem completely identified. Yet whereas the end of the flesh is simply corruption and has no future, man as *sōma* is still 'for the Lord'. What is more, the Christian gospel asserts the incredible fact that 'the Lord is for the body' (that is the meaning of the incarnation and atonement) and that 'God has both raised the Lord and will raise us up through his power' (I Cor. 6.13–14). And this is just what he says in verse 11 – defining this 'power' in terms of the indwelling life-giving energy of the Spirit. Our mortal bodies, our personalities in the sum of all their relationships, *have* a future. What this is is the subject of I Cor. 15, where Paul affirms the resurrection of the body in a way that he never does of the flesh. This resurrection lies still in the future and in its completion is only to be accomplished at the *parousia* or coming of Christ, *not* at the moment of death. For it is a new solidarity whose complete restoration must wait upon the renewing of all things. But it is begun now. The resurrection of the body for Paul starts at baptism (Rom. 6.1–11), when a man is incorporated into the resurrection body of Christ, in which the recreative powers of the new creation are already at work transforming the old. And of this the Spirit is the forestalment and pledge. This is not elaborated in Romans: for its *locus classicus* see II Cor. 4–5. But it is presupposed, not only by his reference to the first-fruits of the Spirit in 8.23, but in his combination of the present indwelling of the Spirit and the future quickening of the body in this passage, which runs literally: 'If Christ is in you, the body is dead because of sin, but the spirit is life because of righteousness.' This could mean that the spirit of man, man as spirit, is alive as opposed to man as body or flesh; but more likely, as in verse 11, that the Spirit is at work giving life (cf. I Cor. 15.45). For if, as a result of your justification, Christ is in you (verse 10), then so too is the Spirit: union with Christ is the way into 'the life of the age to come', whose distinguishing mark is the Spirit.

8.14–17

14 15 For all who are moved by the Spirit of God are sons of God. The Spirit you have received is not a spirit of slavery leading you back into a life of fear, but a Spirit that makes us sons, enabling us to
16 cry 'Abba! Father!' In that cry the Spirit of God joins with our
17 spirit in testifying that we are God's children; and if children, then heirs. We are God's heirs and Christ's fellow-heirs, if we share his sufferings now in order to share his splendour hereafter.

The connection between the Spirit and sonship was already made in Galatians. The argument in Gal. 4.4–7 is closely parallel to that of Romans: 'When the term was completed, God sent his own Son, born of a woman, born under the law, to purchase freedom for the subjects of the law, in order that we might attain the status of sons. To prove that you are sons (*hoti*: 'to declare that'; *not*, as in the RSV, 'because'), God has sent into our hearts the Spirit of his Son, crying "Abba! Father!". You are therefore no longer a slave but a son, and if a son, then also by God's own act heir.' The Spirit is the Spirit that 'makes us sons' (verse 15), because it declares us sons, just as it declared Jesus Son of God at his baptism and at his resurrection (1.4). Though God is the Father of all men, not all men are sons or children of God. This is the consistent view of the Bible: cf. John 1.12, 'He gave the right to become the children of God'. John distinguishes Christ as 'Son' from Christians as 'children' of God. Paul calls Christians both 'sons' (verse 14) and 'children' (verse 16), but always by adoption. Sonship is a spiritual relationship not a natural one. The only exception is in Acts 17.28, where Luke represents Paul as prepared to use the 'we are his offspring' of the heathen poet for apologetic purposes. The New Testament message is: '*Now* are we children of God' (I John 3.2). So here it is the witness of the Spirit and the work of the Spirit alone which pronounces us the children of God – even though our own spirit testifies that this is no strange designation, but that we have 'come home'. This language of 'adoption' is the heart of Paul's gospel – that we are 'sons' not slaves (Gal. 4.7) – even though he was prepared to apply the analogy of slavery even to the new life for a limited purpose (Rom. 6.15–23). And 'if sons, then heirs' (verse 17; cf. again Gal. 4.7 and Mark 12.7 and Heb. 1.2). Hence the Spirit is also 'the pledge that we shall enter upon our heritage' (Eph. 1.14). This idea of an inheritance is always eschatological – corresponding to the promised land of the Old Testament. Talk of 'the Spirit' is also essentially eschatological – for it is the anticipation of the end in the present. Both lead Paul on irresistibly to the hope of glory – the full restoration of the *doxa* or divine splendour lost through sin.

18 For I reckon that the sufferings we now endure bear no comparison with the splendour, as yet unrevealed, which is in store for
19 us. For the created universe waits with eager expectation for
20 God's sons to be revealed. It was made the victim of frustration,
not by its own choice, but because of him who made it so;[a] yet
21 always there was hope, because[b] the universe itself is to be freed
from the shackles of mortality and enter upon the liberty and
22 splendour of the children of God. Up to the present, we know,
the whole created universe groans in all its parts as if in the pangs
23 of childbirth. Not only so, but even we, to whom the Spirit is
given as firstfruits of the harvest to come, are groaning inwardly
while we wait for God to make us his sons and[c] set our whole
24 body free. For we have been saved, though only in hope. Now to
see is no longer to hope: why should a man endure and wait[d] for
25 what he already sees? But if we hope for something we do not yet
see, then, in waiting for it, we show our endurance.

a. *Or* because God subjected it.
b. *Or* with the hope that ...
c. *Some witnesses omit* make us his sons and.
d. *Some witnesses read* why should a man hope ...

Verse 19. The revelation of the sons of God is part of the
parousia, which is always for Paul corporate: it is 'the coming of
our Lord Jesus Christ with all his saints' (I Thess. 3.13). Similarly in Col. 3.4: 'When Christ, who is our life, is manifested,
then you too will be manifested with him in glory.' In Phil.
3.20–21 Paul writes: 'We await the Lord Jesus Christ who will
transfigure the body of our humiliation to be conformed with
the body of his glory.' So in Rom. 8.29 he speaks of Christians
being 'conformed to the likeness of his son'. This end of being
'conformed' is only the final state of the process of being 'transformed into the same image from glory to glory' by the divine
Spirit (II Cor. 3.18), which began when Christ was 'formed'
within us (Gal. 4.19) at baptism – when proleptically we were

101

already invested with the glory which is to be ours (Rom. 8.30). So Paul here takes the traditional apocalyptic imagery of the revealing of the *parousia*, when we shall all be changed in a twinkling of an eye at the last trump (cf. I Cor. 15.51–52), and links it, as he does in II Cor. 3.18, with that regenerating change through the power of the Spirit which Christians, as sons of God, have *already* entered upon at baptism and *into* which (verse 21) the whole creation is to be taken up.

Verse 20. Meanwhile the creation is subjected to 'vanity', as in Ecclesiastes – futility, meaninglessness, failing to reach the goal which gives the whole process significance. Nature was not thus subjected to aimlessness freely or willingly, unlike man, but 'because of him who subjected it'. The reference is clearly to Gen. 3.17 ('accursed shall be the ground on your account'). But does it mean 'because of him who subjected it' (i.e., God who cursed it) or, taking up the 'on your account', because of man, who thus by his action reduced it to its present state? Against most commentators, I believe the reference to Adam is more probable than to God, for Paul's argument seems to run: Creation fell into its thraldom to decay through man's sin (cf. 5.12, 'as through one man'); it can only be freed through man's redemption and by being taken up into his liberation. In each case it is dependent on man, who is the only part of it with free will.

Verse 21. 'The shackles of mortality' or bondage to decay. As 'flesh' the natural creation is, like man, a slave to the powers of disintegration and death (for the 'decay' of man *qua sarx*, the external man, cf. II Cor. 4.16). Its hope is that it shall be included in the redemption and resurrection of existence as *sōma*, creation, that is, as made for God, which is in the first instance the body of *human* existence renewed in and as the body of Christ. *Sōma*, like *sarx*, is essentially a collective term. Hence 'our whole body' (verse 23) – the entire mass of human existence in all its relationships redeemed from the death which is its present doom (7.24). This body will then be a body of 'glory' (cf. I Cor. 15.43; Phil. 3.21), as proleptically in the church, the body of Christ, it already is (Eph. 5.27).

Verse 23. 'The firstfruits' of the Spirit: that is to say, the firstfruits which consist in the Spirit, not the first instalment of the Spirit. In I Cor. 15.20, 23 Christ himself is the firstfruits of the resurrection. The Spirit is the agency through which the resurrection life of Christ himself becomes ours already within this age, because through the Spirit we are in Christ. Here Paul writes 'we wait for God to make us his sons', whereas in verse 15 he had written 'you have received the Spirit which makes us sons'. This is characteristic of the New Testament tension: we *are* children of God, yet always we shall be (I John 3.2).

Verses 24–25. The mention of hope and endurance, like the theme of this entire chapter, picks up the ideas first sketched in 5.2–5. There too the Christian hope is grounded in the gift of the Spirit and in the love of God which makes it all certain. This is what Paul now proceeds to dilate upon – the ultimate reality of God's love behind everything, in which, through the pervasive activity of the Spirit, both faith and hope are grounded.

8.26–30

26 In the same way the Spirit comes to the aid of our weakness. We do not even know how we ought to pray,[a] but through our inar-
27 ticulate groans the Spirit himself is pleading for us, and God who searches our inmost being knows what the Spirit means, because
28 he pleads for God's own people in God's own way; and in everything, as we know, he co-operates for good with those who love
29 God[b] and are called according to his purpose. For God knew his own before ever they were, and also ordained that they should be shaped to the likeness of his Son, that he might be the eldest among a large family of brothers; and it is these, so fore-
30 ordained, whom he has also called. And those whom he called he has justified, and to those whom he justified he has also given his splendour.

a. *Or* what it is right to pray for.
b. *Or* and, as we know, all things work together for good for those who love God; *some witnesses read* and we know God himself co-operates for good with those who love God.

Verses 26–27. 'Through our inarticulate groans the Spirit himself is pleading for us.' In verse 23 he had said 'we groan *even though* we have the Spirit'. The two facts appear purely antithetical. But the Christian life is not merely a matter of patient groaning until.... The pre-possession of the Spirit actually transforms the groanings themselves. They are inarticulate and incoherent, yet the Spirit takes them up and turns them into prayers. Previous English versions attribute the groans or sighs to the Spirit, which is not easily intelligible. Rather, it is our groanings which the Spirit makes his own. He actually uses our groans as prayers and God the searcher of hearts knows what the Spirit means, because he pleads for God's own people in God's own way. Cf. I Cor. 2.10–11: 'For the Spirit explores everything, even the depths of God's own nature. Among men, who knows what a man is but the man's own spirit within him? In the same way, only the Spirit of God knows what God is.' There is an identity between God and the Spirit and an affinity or rapport between the Spirit and our spirits (cf. verse 16) and this is the secret of Christian prayer. Christian prayer has God on both sides of the relationship. 'What the Spirit means' (verse 27) is exactly the same phrase in the Greek that Paul used in verse 6 to describe our attitude in the Spirit, 'the spiritual outlook'. There is no ultimate distinction, because to be in the Spirit is to have the Spirit of God dwelling in us (verse 9).

Verse 28. There is an important dispute about the text at this point. The manuscript support is about equally divided between *panta synergei* (all things work together) and *panta synergei ho theos* (God works all things together). Despite the support of our earliest manuscript ($\mathfrak{P}^{46}$), the shorter text is more likely to be right. There is no reason why *ho theos* (God) should have dropped out, though good reason for adding it as a subject of the verb 'work together' for those who found it impossible to believe that 'all things' could be the subject. Grammatically it could easily be, but it is hard to believe that Paul would have thought in such impersonal terms. Later he goes on to say, not that 'all things work together for good' but that '*in* all things we are supremely victorious through him who loved us' (verse 37).

That is to say, God works with us for victory in everything, if we are in his love. Moreover the point he has just made has concerned the co-operating action of God with us. In fact the noun *synergos* and the verb *synergein* are always used in the New Testament of a person helping another, except in James 2.22, where faith is personified as the subject. The idea of God co-operating with us is thoroughly Pauline, as is our description as 'co-operators with God' (I Cor. 3.9). Almost certainly the scribes who wrote *ho theos* were right in judging that the subject of the verb must be personal and taking *panta* adverbially to mean 'in all things' (as in the RSV text). But did they need to add *ho theos*? I believe Paul wrote simply *synergei* because the subject was already obvious, namely, the Spirit. It is, I think, a great merit of the NEB to knock out the gap between verses 27 and 28 (the RSV actually introduces a new paragraph between them) and restore the continuity of subject: 'He (the Spirit) pleads for God's own people in God's own way. Moreover we know that he co-operates for good in *every* way (and not only in prayer) with those who love God and are called according to his purpose.' There is an interesting parallel for this usage in the Jewish work *The Testaments of the Twelve Patriarchs*: 'The spirit of love patiently co-operates with the law of God for the salvation of men' (Gad 4.7).

'Those who love God' are not simply any who have love in their hearts but, as Paul goes on to draw out in verse 29, those whom God has brought within his election love – just as in Luke 2.14 the promise of peace on earth is not to men of good will (AV), but to men of his good pleasure. Cf. Eph. 1.5: 'He destined us – such was his will and pleasure – to be accepted as his sons through Jesus Christ.' So here Paul links God's love, his purpose, his calling, his foreknowledge, his predestination and our sonship. This 'foreknowledge' is not knowledge of facts about the future (which Paul never asserts), but the deep personal knowledge such as the Old Testament predicates of God towards Israel his elect or his servants the prophets, particularly in Jer. 1.5 (which Paul applied to himself in Gal. 1.15): 'Before I formed you in the womb I knew you for my own; before you were born I consecrated you, I appointed you a prophet to the nations.' So all God's people, and not only the prophets, are now in the position of being thus 'known' and elected.

Verse 30. Paul summarizes the stages in the process of salvation described in the epistle: foreordination (corresponding to the 'set apart' of 1.1), calling (corresponding to the 'called' of 1.6), justification (the theme of 1.16–4.25) and glorification (the theme of 5–8). Of the final stage, 'he has glorified us', Denney wrote: 'The tense of this last word is amazing. It is the most daring anticipation of faith that even the New Testament contains.' It propels Paul into his final peroration.

8.31–39

---

31 With all this in mind, what are we to say? If God is on our side,
32 who is against us? He did not spare his own Son, but surrendered him for us all; and with this gift how can he fail to lavish upon us
33 all he has to give? Who will be the accuser of God's chosen ones?
34 It is God who pronounces acquittal: then who can condemn? It is Christ – Christ who died, and, more than that, was raised from the dead – who is at God's right hand, and indeed pleads our
35 cause.[a] Then what can separate us from the love of Christ? Can affliction or hardship? Can persecution, hunger, nakedness, peril, or the sword? 'We are being done to death for thy sake all
36 day long,' as Scripture says; 'we have been treated like sheep for
37 slaughter' – and yet, in spite of all, overwhelming victory is ours
38 through him who loved us. For I am convinced that there is nothing in death or life, in the realm of spirits or superhuman powers, in the world as it is or the world as it shall be, in the
39 forces of the universe, in heights or depths – nothing in all creation that can separate us from the love of God in Christ Jesus our Lord.

a. *Or* Who will be the accuser of God's chosen ones? Will it be God himself? No, he it is who pronounces acquittal. Who will be the judge to condemn? Will it be Christ – he who died, and, more than that, ... right hand? No, he it is who pleads our cause.

Thus ends perhaps the greatest chapter in the New Testament. It speaks for itself or not at all. All commentary is bathos – like trying to describe the Ninth Symphony in words. I will confine myself to a few small points.

Verse 32. 'His own son' picks up the reference to 'his son' in verse 2. But here there is a clear echo also of Gen. 22.16, 'You have not withheld your son, your only son' – the sole reference to this incident in Abraham's life in Paul's writings. God 'gave him up' is, as Barth comments, the same verb used in 1.24, 26, 28 of God giving men up to the effects of their own passions.

'How will he not with him give us all things?' The NEB translates 'with this gift': with him everything is included, or, as Denney puts it, 'When God gives us his Son he gives us the world'. But it is just possible that the 'with' (*syn*) may have a more pregnant meaning. It is when we are 'with him' or 'in him' that everything can be ours. This is Paul's regular use of *syn*, to mean not 'as well as' but 'in union with'. It is 'with Christ', in the body of Christ, as members of the 'large family of brothers' (verse 29), that 'all things are ours'. We may compare the series of compound verbs beginning with *syn-* in the Greek of verse 17: 'Fellow heirs of Christ if indeed we suffer with him that we may be glorified together' (cf. also 6.3–8; Eph. 2.5–6; 3.6; Col. 2.12–13). Moreover this sense of *syn* as 'one with him' fits the impossibility of severance which follows: 'Then what can separate us from the love of Christ?' (cf. Eph. 2.12–13, where the opposite of 'separate from Christ' is 'in Christ'). But the non-pregnant meaning of 'with' is all we can be sure of.

Verse 33. Paul returns once more to the forensic metaphor of accusation at court, acquittal and condemnation, reminding us of the book of Job. Christians are outside the range of all this now. As dead men there is for them no more interrogation (6.7), as acquitted men no more condemnation (8.2).

It is possible by punctuating it differently, with the NEB margin, to take it as a series of rhetorical questions expecting the answer, No. 'Who will be the accuser? Is it God, the very one who pronounces acquittal? Who will be the judge to condemn? Will it be Christ, who died and rose and actually pleads our cause? Then what can separate us? Can affliction, etc. . .? No, in all these we have overwhelming victory.' This gives good sense, though it involves an awkward splitting up of the quotation from Isa. 50.8–9 ('It is God who pronounces acquittal: then who can condemn?'); but in Paul's use of scripture this is not fatal. It is adopted by the RSV text and Barrett, though Cranfield here sides with the NEB text.

Verse 35. This is the 'exultation even in our present sufferings' of which Paul spoke in 5.3, and which like everything else in 5.1–5 here finds its elaboration and climax. Similarly the aorist 'loved us' in verse 37 has the same backward reference. The ground of victory is not the love of God in general but the specific act of God in Christ which proved the love he has for us (5.8). This in turn leads up to the final phrase in verse 39: 'the love of God in Christ Jesus our Lord' – the ultimate definition and vindication of what love means.

So we leave Paul on the crest of the wave that has borne him on from 5.1. From now the descent begins – and we can go more quickly.

Chapters 9–11

Yet the next stage is not what we should expect. Instead of passing to the direct corollary of all this, as in the resounding 'therefore' of Eph. 4.1, which marks the moral section of the epistle off from the doctrinal, Paul now enters in chapters 9–11 upon what reads like an excursus and *could* be detached from the rest without affecting its argument and structure. 12.1 would follow perfectly well on 8.39. In fact it is possibly an independent unit which Paul has introduced here. As Dodd says, 'We get the impression that we are listening to Paul preaching. . . . It is the kind of sermon that Paul must often have had occasion to deliver, in defining his attitude to what we may call the Jewish question. It is quite possible that he kept by him a manuscript of such a sermon, for use as occasion demanded, and inserted it here.'

But others (e.g., most recently, K. Stendahl, *Paul among Jews and Gentiles*, 1977) have argued that it represents the point and climax of the whole epistle. Structurally it is difficult to believe this, but if it is an excursus it is closely related to the themes of the first half of the letter. In fact it is really a detailed expansion of the issues raised and adumbrated in chapter 3:

3.1–2 = 9.1–5 (the privileges of the Jews)

3.3–4 = 9.6–13 (the faithlessness of the Jews does not mean God's promise has failed)

3.5–6 = 9.14–18 (his judgment of some does not mean that he is unjust)

3.7–8 = 9.19–29 (but is it not unfair of him then to find fault? No)

3.9–20 = 9.30–33 (what then? Just what scripture says: as far as legal righteousness is concerned the Jews have failed as hopelessly as the Gentiles)

3.21–28 = 10 (but there is a righteousness of God that comes by faith, open to all without distinction)

3.29–31 = 11 (God is the God neither of Jew nor of Gentile alone: he wills to save both and thus vindicate his ways to man).

The whole section is in effect the answer to the question in 3.9, which ever way it is translated: 'Are we Jews any better off?' or 'Are we Jews any worse off?' And the answer in either case is 'No, not at all'. The Jews have immense privileges (9.4–5): but these have secured them no advantage. In fact, if anything, the advantage lies with the Gentiles, for 'Gentiles, who made no effort after righteousness, nevertheless achieved it, a righteousness based on faith; whereas Israel made great efforts after a law of righteousness, but never attained to it' (9.30–31). And yet this is only a temporary lead – for 'the whole of Israel will be saved' (11.26). Just as there is no distinction in sin, so there will be none in salvation: 'For in making all mankind prisoners to disobedience, God's purpose was to show mercy to all mankind' (11.32).

The real difference in this section – which gives it its difference of tone and style – is that Paul is here seeing the problem not primarily in terms of theology but of history. It is not only that the Jews have no advantage in theory (that he has done his best to explain); but in practice also the Christian gospel, which he is so concerned to show is in line with the promises of God, is excluding all but a few of his chosen people. How can these things be? The problem is one that Paul, as a Jew, feels at the most intensely personal level: the Jewish question is not for him a mere theologoumenon. And it is a problem moreover which he and 'his gospel' have done more than any other single factor to create. And so little is he content with a purely theoretical answer to this question, that his solution is in fact the opposite of that which *a priori* his theology would dictate. The order of theology was 'to the Jew first and also to the Greek' (1.16); the order of history has turned out to be 'to the Gentile first and also to the Jew' (11.25–26).

9.1–5

The Purpose of God in History

9 I am speaking the truth as a Christian, and my own conscience,
2 enlightened by the Holy Spirit, assures me it is no lie: in my heart
3 there is great grief and unceasing sorrow. For I could even pray
to be outcast from Christ myself for the sake of my brothers, my
4 natural kinsfolk. They are Israelites: they were made God's sons;
theirs is the splendour of the divine presence, theirs the coven-
5 ants, the law, the temple worship, and the promises. Theirs are
the patriarchs, and from them, in natural descent, sprang the

Messiah.[a] May God, supreme above all, be blessed for ever![b]
Amen.

a *Greek* Christ.
b *Or* sprang the Messiah, supreme above all, God blessed for ever; *or* sprang the
Messiah, who is supreme above all. Blessed be God for ever!

Paul starts from the glory that makes the tragedy what it is.

Verse 5 contains the only clear use in Paul of *ho christos*, the
Christ, as a title and not a proper name. But immediately after it
we have a vexed question of punctuation. Sanday and Headlam
begin their (admirable) excursus on it with the ominous remark:
'The interpretation of Rom. 9.5 has probably been discussed at
greater length than that of any other verse of the New Testament', and since then the discussion has certainly not stopped.
(See especially: R. E. Brown, 'Does the New Testament call
Jesus God?' in *Jesus, God and Man*, 1968, pp. 20–22, and B.
Metzger, 'The Punctuation of Romans 9.5', in ed., B. Lindars
and S. S. Smalley, *Christ and Spirit in the New Testament*, 1973,
pp. 95–112). Literally and without punctuation the words run:
'and of whom is the Christ according to the flesh who is God
over all blessed for ever amen'. There are other minor variations, but two main choices: (*a*) to put a comma after 'according
to the flesh' and to refer 'who is God over all' to Christ (RV
text, RSV margin, NEB margin) or (*b*) to put a full-stop after
'according to the flesh' and then start again: 'He who is God
over all be blessed for ever' (RV margin, RSV text, NEB text).
There was no punctuation in the original manuscript, so it is
simply a question of weighing up probabilities.

Grammatically there is almost everything to be said for (*a*). If
Paul had wanted to say, 'Blessed be God who is over all' he
would naturally have begun with the word 'blessed' (as in English, and as in II Cor. 1.3; Eph. 1.3). The relative 'who is'
would naturally refer back, and there is a close parallel in II
Cor. 11.31: 'The God and Father of the Lord Jesus, who is
blessed for ever, knows that I do not lie' (though cf. John 3.21,
where 'he who is of the earth' refers forward). Yet in II Cor.
11.31 'he who is blessed for ever' refers not to Christ but to

111

God, and therein lies the *theological* difficulty. Paul never else-where calls Christ 'God', let alone 'God over all': Christ is regularly subordinated to God (I Cor. 11.3, 'the head of Christ is God'; 15.28, the subjection of the Son to Father). Some would argue that he comes so near it as to make little difference. But Denney says: 'If we ask ourselves point blank, whether Paul, as we know his mind from his epistles, would express his sense of Christ's greatness by calling him God blessed for ever, it seems to me almost impossible to answer in the affirmative.' If we take it the other way, with a full-stop after 'according to the flesh', the doxology may seem to us redundant; but it is what Paul as a pious Jew often inserts. Romans 1.25 is a good example: 'They ... offered reverence and worship to created things instead of to the Creator' – and he adds: 'who is blessed for ever; amen'.

Sanday and Headlam and most recently Metzger argue strongly for referring *theos* (God) to Christ, and Brown and Nygren agree. But Denney and Dodd, Bultmann, Knox and Vincent Taylor are against them, as are most modern versions (Moffatt, Goodspeed, RSV, NEB, the Good News Bible, though not the Jerusalem Bible) and I myself as a translator of the NEB cast my vote for (*b*). But I confess that I am shaken. Barrett adopts (*b*) in his translation, but sits on the fence in his commentary.

It is just worth mentioning an attractive emendation which has much to commend it except manuscript support: for *ho ōn* read *hōn ho*: 'Whose are the patriarchs, etc., of whom is the Messiah by natural descent, and *whose is the* one true God?' In this case, the climax of the privileges of Israel is the fact that God said: 'I will be their God and they shall be my people' (Jer. 31.33, etc.). Despite absence of manuscript evidence, it is not impossible that this is what Paul dictated. Yet Metzger is against it on several grammatical grounds, but more importantly because it contradicts 3.29: 'Is God the God of the Jews only? Is he not the God of Gentiles also? Yes, of Gentiles also.'

6   It is impossible that the word of God should have proved false.
7   For not all descendants of Israel are truly Israel, nor, because they are Abraham's offspring, are they all his true children;[a] but, in the words of Scripture, 'Through the line of Isaac your post-
8   erity shall be traced.'[b] That is to say, it is not those born in the course of nature who are children of God; it is the children born through God's promise who are reckoned as Abraham's descen-
9   dants. For the promise runs: 'At the time fixed I will come, and Sarah shall have a son.'
10   But that is not all, for Rebekah's children had one and the
11   same father, our ancestor, Isaac; and yet, in order that God's selective purpose might stand, based not upon men's deeds but
12   upon the call of God, she was told, even before they were born, when they had as yet done nothing, good or ill, 'The elder shall
13   be servant to the younger'; and that accords with the text of Scripture, 'Jacob I loved and Esau I hated.'

a. *Or* all children of God.
b. *Or* God's call shall be for your descendants in the line of Isaac.

But if these promises were made to Israel, doesn't that mean that God's word has failed? No. As Dodd puts it in a section of admirable commentary, 'His promise to bless "Israel", his chosen people, certainly holds good; but it is for him to decide with absolute freedom who shall constitute that chosen people. If he chooses to reject the Jews and to elect Gentiles, then the true "Israel" is composed of those whom he elects'. And for this Paul appeals to a principle which every Jew would admit – the term 'children of Abraham' does not mean everyone physically descended from Abraham. 'Ishmael was a child of Abraham, but no Jew believed' (or we may add, believes) 'that the Arabs, his descendants, were within the covenant'. Again, the principle of selection does not stop there. For even among the sons of Isaac, the child of promise, there was choice and rejection. Again every Jew must admit this – otherwise Jews and Edomites would be on the same footing. And this second illustration, says Paul, is especially instructive. In the first instance it could be argued that the principle of selection was based on parentage – Ishmael after all was the illegitimate son of a slave-girl. But the two sons of Isaac and Rebecca had the same father and the same mother. In fact they were twins, born under exactly the same star, and even before they were born, before they had done anything good or bad, a selection was made between them. This leads Paul into his main theme that election is grounded solely in the sovereign call of God and in nothing that man does. This will be important for him, as it shows that the principle of exclusion and the principle of subsequent inclusion are the same: neither is dependent on 'works', each is based wholly and absolutely in the graciousness and mercy of God.

But this is going too far ahead. Mercy, did you say? But the process looks just the opposite, rank injustice.

To this Paul has two replies. The first is in 9.14–21, the second in 9.22–29.

9.14–29

14 What shall we say to that? Is God to be charged with injustice?
15 By no means. For he says to Moses, 'Where I show mercy, I will
16 show mercy, and where I pity, I will pity.' Thus it does not
17 depend on man's will or effort, but on God's mercy. For Scripture says to Pharaoh, 'I have raised you up for this very purpose, to exhibit my power in my dealings with you, and to spread my
18 fame over all the world.' Thus he not only shows mercy as he chooses, but also makes men stubborn as he chooses.

19 You will say, 'Then why does God blame a man? For who can
20 resist his will?' Who are you, sir, to answer God back? Can the pot speak to the potter and say, 'Why did you make me like this?'
21 Surely the potter can do what he likes with the clay. Is he not free

114

to make out of the same lump two vessels, one to be treasured, the other for common use?

22 But what if God, desiring to exhibit[a] his retribution at work and to make his power known, tolerated very patiently those
23 vessels which were objects of retribution due for destruction, and did so in order to make known the full wealth of his splendour upon vessels which were objects of mercy, and which from the first had been prepared for this splendour?

24 Such vessels are we, whom he has called from among Gentiles
25 as well as Jews, as it says in the Book of Hosea: 'Those who were not my people I will call My People, and the unloved nation I will
26 call My Beloved. For in the very place where they were told "you are no people of mine", they shall be called Sons of the living
27 God.' But Isaiah makes this proclamation about Israel: 'Though the Israelites be countless as the sands of the sea, it is but a
28 remnant that shall be saved; for the Lord's sentence on the land
29 will be summary and final'; as also he said previously, 'If the Lord of Hosts had not left us the mere germ of a nation, we should have become like Sodom, and no better than Gomorrah.'

a *Or* although he had the will to exhibit. . . .

Verses 14–21. Injustice is not a category you can apply to God: for that would be to judge him by something outside his own will, to subordinate him to a external standard of your own selection – and then he would cease to be God. His own 'good pleasure' is the ultimate reality, and it is absolute and impartial. As Creator he has sovereign rights over his creation. But, says the objector, isn't this pure determinism? Doesn't it destroy freedom and responsibility? Again, as in chapter 3, Paul does not give a rational answer to a reasonable objection. From what he has said in chapters 1 and 2 and goes on to say in 9.30–10.21 it is certain that he does not teach a doctrine of the divine sovereignty which leaves men without choice or responsibility for their actions – in fact just the opposite. But he refuses to treat the objection that this is what he is saying as more than a sophistication – and thereby leaves his conception of God's working wide open to misunderstanding. Indeed, he positively invites it by the analogy that he uses. He *could* have drawn one

115

from the realm of personal relationships, to show how grace need not be antithetical to freedom. He could have appealed to our experience of human love. For when we are under the constraint of love, however overwhelming, it is not a compulsion that takes away our freedom. On the contrary, we never feel more utterly free than when we yield ourselves in complete self-giving to one whom we really love. Love as love has the power to move only what retains complete freedom to refuse to be moved. You cannot move a chair by loving it, only a person. And the purer and more unconditional the love, the greater the degree of freedom it presupposes and demands, not the less. (On this see the classic study by John Oman, *Grace and Personality*, 1917, and also the remarkable passage in Kierkegaard's *Journals*, ET, excerpt 616, p. 180, on omnipotence being required to make men free.) But Paul simply quashes the objector with an analogy from a purely instrumental relationship, which confirms while it dismisses all his opponent's worst suspicions. But we must not press Paul's analogies, here or elsewhere. He has brought it in for one purpose only, to show that the Creator has absolute freedom over his creatures: he is not concerned at this point to find one which will also safeguard *their* freedom. For this is immaterial in the present context, and the objector's raising of it is a red herring.

But this is not in fact the only answer that Paul has. God's will, he says, *could* be arbitrary, not only in the sense that he alone disposes it, but in the sense that he disposes it according to whim: and if that *were* so we should have no right to object any more than the pot has to the potter. Yet, he goes on, we have reason to think that in fact it is not purely arbitrary – and he proceeds to state the reason in terms of the very analogy that seemed so unpromising – the freedom of the potter to make out of the same lump two vessels, one to be treasured, the other for common use (verse 21). For the background cf. again Wisd. 15.7 of a human potter: 'Out of the self-same clay he fashions without distinction the pots that are to serve for honourable uses and the opposite; and what the purpose of each one is to be, the moulder of the clay decides.'

Verses 22–29. '*But* what if God. . . .' Neither the AV, RV,
RSV nor other modern versions translate the 'but'. It is a merit
again of the NEB that not only does it do so, but it starts a new
paragraph. For this is a new and antithetical point. And since
this paragraph has given rise to more misrepresentation and
bad theology than any other – or let us say as much bad theology as any other – it is worth going into its logic in some detail.

God, Paul has just said, is not to be charged with injustice
even if no principle can be seen in his dealings. *But* in fact, so far
from being unjust, his record with men reveals precisely the
opposite quality. There *is* a principle and it is one of quite
unmerited mercy.

The understanding of this passage depends on keeping in
mind its background in Jer. 18.1–11: 'So I went down to the
potter's house, and found him working at the wheel. Now and
then a vessel he was making out of the clay would be spoilt in his
hands, and then he would start again and mould it into another
vessel to his liking. Then the word of the Lord came to me:
"Can I not deal with you, Israel", says the Lord, "as the potter
deals with his clay? You are clay in my hands like the clay in his,
O house of Israel".' In other words God has sovereign freedom
over his chosen vessel, and whenever he likes he can remould it
to his heart's desire. But, says Paul, this is not what God has
done; he has *not* scrapped the vessel he is making, reworked the
clay and started again; he has endured with incredible patience
vessels which have become fit only to be smashed. Why did he
do it? For two reasons: (*a*) to demonstrate the power of his
orgē, his wrath (verse 22) and (*b*) to reveal the full scope of his
glory (verse 23). But why does (*a*) show his patience, his long-
heartedness? So difficult does this seem that many have taken
the participle 'desiring to' as concessive, as in the NEB margin:
'although he had the will to exhibit'. In other words, What if
God, though he wished to let fly, in fact showed himself incred-
ibly long-suffering? This is superficially easier, though it runs
into other difficulties – e.g., the fact that Paul goes on '*and* in
order that' as though he had already indicated one purpose of
God's action. This grammatical difficulty would not be decisive

in a writer like Paul. But in fact the larger context both of the passage and of the epistle I believe are against this interpretation (Barrett is good at this point).

It is to be observed that there is a close parallel between verses 22–23 and verse 17 above. In verses 14–18 Paul is illustrating from Old Testament history the absolute impartiality of God. God, he says, makes use equally of what (in terms of the potter analogy) Paul is to call vessels of mercy and vessels of wrath. As an example of the former he cites Moses (the representative of God's people) and of the latter Pharaoh (the representative of God's enemies). Instead of simply liquidating Pharaoh, God used him – in fact he himself actually 'raised him up'. And he used him (verse 17) for two purposes, to give a demonstration of his power and to proclaim his name through all the earth.

Now, says Paul, this is what is happening again. Only this time the roles ironically are reversed. Israel now represents the vessel of his wrath (standing where Pharaoh did), the Gentiles the vessel of his mercy. But, just as God did not simply rub out Pharaoh, so now he has not simply rubbed out Israel though this indeed is all that Israel has deserved. He has been using Israel – and that again for the very two purposes for which he used Pharaoh: (*a*) as a demonstration, a working model, of his wrath, and (*b*) as the occasion for proclaiming his glory to all nations. That is to say, he has kept Israel on the stocks all this time because (not although) he wanted to give a demonstration of how his *orgē* operates, deliberately allowing rejection of God to reach its full fruiting, its end-term, instead of cutting it short, as he would surely have done had not he been so long-suffering. For this demonstration of his 'wrath' is only, as we have seen (1.17–18), the other aspect, the dark side or shadow, of the demonstration of his 'righteousness', on which Paul has expatiated in 3.25–26. It is precisely part of God's mercy that his *orgē* should be fully *revealed*; and this is why he 'passed over former sins' (3.25), this is why with such tolerance and patience he 'laid off' punishing the Jews earlier (2.4). If he had not shown such forbearance then, there would be no effects of retribution to be

118

seen now, and therefore no demonstration of his 'righteous-ness'.

This interpretation of 'desiring', not as concessive but as ex-pressing the purpose of God in 'enduring' the Jews, fits, I believe, much better with the tenor of the passage and with the profound interpretation of *orgē* throughout the epistle. If we say that *although* God would have liked to have let fly he neverthe-less showed great long-suffering, we fall into a superficial anti-thesis of mercy and anger in God which Paul never counte-nances.

Paul's argument therefore is that there is no injustice (*adikia*) with God (verse 14). On the contrary, all his dealings are a demonstration of his righteousness (*dikaiosynē*), and the pat-tern of that righteousness is always 'wrath for the ends of mercy' (cf. the conclusion of the whole section in 11.32). And this mercy comes to direct expression in the second purpose in God's persistence with the Jews – namely, that through their hardening salvation might come to the Gentiles. The process by which this comes about is to be the theme of chapter 11. Mean-while, in chapter 10, he has something else to fix – namely, Israel's responsibility for all this.

But before that, in verses 24–29, he rounds off his previous argument in his usual way – with an appeal to scripture, the final arbiter. First he appeals to Hosea, to prove the unmerited generosity of God to those who are not 'his people' (though originally these words were addressed to Israel!), and then to Isaiah, to show how the fact that a mere remnant of Israel has been saved is *not* against God's purposes, but exactly what he said would happen. God had to be severe. Yet even this severity reveals his mercy. For the point of Paul's final quotation, from Isa. 1.9, is not merely (as in the original) that *only* a remnant has been left, but that through sheer grace a germ *has* survived. Israel has not been utterly wiped out like Sodom and Gomor-rah. Thus even the driblet of Jews who have entered the prom-ises is a sign not of God's failure and injustice, but of his mercy. For after Israel's history you had no right to expect even that.

If this is the logic of this passage, it is ironical indeed that it should have been made the basis for precisely the opposite doctrine of God, namely, that of a celestial Mikado who has deliberately and gleefully created half mankind for the purpose of consigning them to damnation. But, quite apart from the fact that Paul is here out to prove the sheer graciousness of God, he never says that *God has created* the vessels for retribution. They have *become spoiled* in his hand, like the potter's clay in Jeremiah. They have become 'vessels of wrath', just as human nature created by God as good has become 'sinful flesh'. He does not say that God has fitted them for destruction, as he does say that God has prepared the others for glory: they have become fit only for destruction. (There is a good discussion of this imbalance from the doctrinal point of view in Brunner's *Christian Doctrine of God*, 1949, p. 323–34.)

A doctrine of double predestination has been read into the passage with a ruthless logic that ends by attributing to Paul the very opposite of what he is intending. Yet there is no doubt that Paul by refusing to guard his flank and by deliberately throwing down the offensive metaphor of the potter has laid himself open to such misunderstanding. It is a warning not to treat the objections of unbelief too cavalierly, even if one thinks them insincere.

But now we come to the other side of the coin. Paul has vindicated the sovereignty of God: next he must fix the responsibility of man. And that responsibility lies squarely on Israel: its unbelief was its own fault, not a failure of God's promises.

9.30–10.21

---

30 Then what are we to say? That Gentiles, who made no effort after righteousness, nevertheless achieved it, a righteousness
31 based on faith; whereas Israel made great efforts after a law of
32 righteousness, but never attained to it. Why was this? Because

their efforts were not based on faith, but (as they supposed) on
33 deeds. They stumbled over the 'stumbling-stone' mentioned in
Scripture: 'Here I lay in Zion a stumbling-stone and a rock to
trip them up; but he who has faith in him will not be put to
shame.'

10 Brothers, my deepest desire and my prayer to God is for their
2 salvation. To their zeal for God I can testify; but it is an ill-
3 informed zeal. For they ignore God's way of righteousness, and
try to set up their own, and therefore they have not submitted
4 themselves to God's righteousness. For Christ ends the law and
brings righteousness for everyone who has faith.[a]

5 Of legal righteousness Moses writes, 'The man who does this
6 shall gain life by it.' But the righteousness that comes by faith
says, 'Do not say to yourself, "Who can go up to heaven?" ' (that
7 is to bring Christ down), 'or, "Who can go down to the abyss?" '
8 (to bring Christ up from the dead). But what does it say? 'The
word is near you: it is upon your lips and in your heart.' This
9 means the word of faith which we proclaim. If on your lips is the
confession, 'Jesus is Lord', and in your heart the faith that God
10 raised him from the dead, then you will find salvation. For the
faith that leads to righteousness is in the heart, and the confession that leads to salvation is upon the lips.

11 Scripture says, 'Everyone who has faith in him will be saved
12 from shame' – everyone: there is no distinction between Jew and
Greek, because the same Lord is Lord of all, and is rich enough
13 for the need of all who invoke him. For everyone, as it says again
– 'everyone who invokes the name of the Lord will be saved'.
14 How could they invoke one in whom they had no faith? And how
could they have faith in one they had never heard of? And how
15 hear without someone to spread the news? And how could anyone spread the news without a commission to do so? And that is
what Scripture affirms: 'How welcome are the feet of the messengers of good news!'

16 But not all have responded to the good news. For Isaiah says,
17 'Lord, who has believed our message?' We conclude that faith is
awakened by the message, and the message that awakens it
comes through the word of Christ.

18 But, I ask, can it be that they never heard it? Of course they
did: 'Their voice has sounded all over the earth, and their words
19 to the bounds of the inhabited world.' But, I ask again, can it be
that Israel failed to recognize the message? In reply, I first cite
Moses, who says, 'I will use a nation that is no nation to stir your

20   envy, and a foolish nation to rouse your anger.' But Isaiah is still more daring: 'I was found', he says, 'by those who were not looking for me; I was clearly shown to those who never asked

21   about me'; while to Israel he says, 'All day long I have stretched out my hands to an unruly and recalcitrant people.'

a. Or Christ is the end of the law as a way to righteousness for everyone who has faith.

Israel with the law has not attained righteousness (i.e., again, not morality but acceptance by God, almost salvation); the Gentiles without it have. Once more, is not that utterly arbitrary and unjust? It would be, says Paul, were it not for one thing that gives the clue. As Dodd puts it, 'The paradoxical state of affairs exhibited in the Christian church is absolutely inexplicable except by the inscrutable fiat of God, *unless* the principle of justification by grace through faith is accepted. The acceptance of that principle at once makes it possible to give an ethical account of the matter.' It is not divine arbitrariness which has produced this paradoxical result, but human failure. The Jews fell down on the decisive insight – that God-acceptedness rests not on attainment, on 'making good their own way', but on unqualified reliance on him. And the reason why Jew and Gentile are in exactly the same position is that Christ has shown this to be the *only* consideration: literally nothing else matters. He is the end of law as a means of righteousness to everyone who has faith – or he is the end of law and brings righteousness to everyone who has faith. That is the positive message of this section – a repetition of the gospel of chapter 3 that justification is by faith alone.

But the underlying question is: 'How on earth were the Jews to know this and how can they be held responsible for their error?' (Dodd). The answer is, again as in 3.21, that this righteousness of God is 'attested by the law and the prophets'. It was all there in the Old Testament if they had had the eyes to see it. For the Old Testament is a witness not only to what Paul calls 'the righteousness of law' (i.e., of works) but also to 'the righteousness of faith'. And he proceeds to show this by drawing attention to the fact that within the Mosaic law there are two quite different strands (again what critically we should distinguish as P and D). The first (verse 5), the Levitical code, is concerned with observance, with correct performance. That is what it says in Lev. 18.5: 'The good life is in the performance.' But (verses 6–8) in the Deuteronomic code there is a more inward conception: 'The good life is in personal relationship with God.' And this is nothing recondite or external to man: it is internal to the very structure of human existence (Deut. 30.11–14). Then (verse 9), by an interpretation which stretches somewhat the bounds of strict exegesis, Paul proceeds to say what he thinks this passage really means. The personal relationship is the relationship of faith, and the meaning of faith is unconditional trust in the living lordship of Christ. The Christ figure is not now something remote or speculative. 'There is no need for you to say, Who will go up into heaven? Heaven has come down to you; Christ has come down and lived among men. There is no need to search the hidden places of the deep. Christ has risen. There is no need therefore to seek the living among the dead' (Sanday and Headlam's paraphrase). Or, as Dodd puts it: 'Christ is not an inaccessible heavenly figure (like the apocalyptic Messiah of Judaism), nor yet a dead prophet (as the Jews thought), but the living Lord of his people, always near'. And Paul goes on (verse 13), in a way that indicates very clearly that what he means by 'Lord' is nothing derived, as used to be asserted, from the Hellenistic mysteries, to quote an Old Testament reference to 'the Lord', which he interprets unhesitatingly as alluding to Christ: 'Everyone who invokes the Lord by name shall be saved' (Joel 2.32).

This whole passage is important for Paul's understanding of faith. It is the only one that appears to equate faith with belief in a proposition: 'If on your lips is the confession, "Jesus is Lord", and in your heart the faith that God raised him from the dead, then you will find salvation' (verse 9). Martin Buber in his book *Two Types of Faith* (1951) on the basis of this accused Paul and Christianity of having introduced a wholly new conception of faith – belief in propositions and events and therefore in a creed

123

– which was foreign to the true Hebraic understanding of faith, as simple trust, common to the prophets and to Jesus. But, as Paul's quotation from the prophets (Isa. 28.16) in verse 11 makes clear, faith for him is still utterly personal trust: 'Everyone who has faith in him will be saved from shame.' This faith or trust can be expressed equally well as faith in God who raises, and has raised Jesus, from the dead (4.24) or as faith in Jesus (3.25) raised from the dead, i.e., faith in Christ as a living presence and Lord. And both of these find expression in verse 9, which summarizes the content of the Christian preaching.

But it is all very well for Paul to say that all the Jew had to do was to put his trust in God thus defined. But how could he know? The argument that follows in verses 14–21 is of the same kind that Paul used against the Jewish position in chapters 2–3, as he knocks down one prop of excuse after another on which they might rely. The technique is that of the diatribe, of rapid question and answer. I would quote Sanday and Headlam's excellent paraphrase at this point: ' "But how can men believe the Gospel unless it has been fully preached?" (verse 14). *Answer*: "It has been preached, as Isaiah foretold" (verse 15). "Yet, all have not accepted it" (verse 16). *Answer*: "That does not prove that it was not preached. Isaiah foretold also this neglect of the message" (verses 16–17). "But perhaps the Jews did not hear" (verse 18). *Answer*: "Impossible. The Gospel has been preached everywhere". "But perhaps they did not understand" (verse 19). *Answer*: "That again is impossible. The Gentiles, a people without any real knowledge, have understood. The real fact is that they were a disobedient, self-willed people" (verses 19–21).' Paul's immediate reference is to the Christian preaching and to the chances the Jews of his generation had to respond to it. But he substantiates his charge by saying that it has always been the same. Scripture shows it, though in order to show it scripture has sometimes to be pressed pretty hard – for example in verse 18, where the quotation from Ps. 19.4, 'their voice has sounded all over the earth, and their words to the bounds of the inhabited world', referred originally not to preachers of the gospel but to the heavenly bodies which

124

declare the glory of God. The quotation in verse 15 too is difficult. Literally, as in the RSV's 'as it is written, "How beautiful are the feet of those who bring good news!" ', it appears to do no more than re-express Paul's point in scriptural terms. But in fact it *makes* his point, and is the linchpin of his whole argument. For it provides the answer to the final question – and so to the whole series. How could they have heard unless there had been someone to tell them? But that is what scripture puts beyond doubt: there *were* people to tell them, 'for it says ...'. 'As it is written' is here a very condensed expression and must mean: 'Yes, but this is exactly what the Bible says'. There *were* commissioned agents to spread the news. Therefore there is no excuse.

Paul's appeal to scripture may make anyone with any critical principles wince a bit. But it is important to notice that at a deeper level it is by no means arbitrary. Throughout this passage (and it is not untypical) the appeal has been almost wholly to one strain of scripture, namely to Deuteronomy and II and III Isaiah. It is here that the gospel before Christ is most explicitly revealed, and the messengers upon the mountains are those who bring the news of that deliverance from exile which is the prototype of the Christian message. *Basically* Paul's appeal to scripture is a profoundly spiritual one, going unerringly to the heart of the Old Testament as a Christian book. His *technique* of exegesis shows him to be a man of his age. But his insights into what the Old Testament is about possess an abiding validity. (On all this, cf. Dodd, *According to the Scriptures*, 1952.)

So we pass to the final chapter of this essay in theodicy. The whole might be entitled 'the justification of God'. The first half of the argument has been negative. God has not failed. His sovereignty is not impugned (9.6–29), nor is his morality (9.30–10.21): he is not to be blamed for the failure of the Jews. But now Paul turns to the positive side. It is not merely that God is not to be blamed: on the contrary, through all this human failure his saving purpose is actually being accomplished. It is to the tracing of this purpose that Paul now addresses himself. The argument once again falls into three divisions –

two negative and one positive. The failure of Israel has not been total (11.1–10); it has not been final (11.11–24); and it will be shown to be the means ultimately to the total restoration not only of Israel but of the world (11.25–36).

11.1–36

---

11   I ask then, has God rejected his people? I cannot believe it! I am an Israelite myself, of the stock of Abraham, of the tribe of
2   Benjamin. No! God has not rejected the people which he acknowledged of old as his own. You know (do you not?) what Scripture says in the story of Elijah – how Elijah pleads with God
3   against Israel: 'Lord, they have killed thy prophets, they have overthrown thine altars, and I alone am left, and they are seeking
4   my life.' But what does the oracle say to him? 'I have left myself
5   seven thousand men who have not done homage to Baal.' In just the same way at the present time a 'remnant' has come into
6   being, selected by the grace of God. But if it is by grace, then it does not rest on deeds done, or grace would cease to be grace.
7   What follows? What Israel sought, Israel has not achieved, but the selected few have achieved it. The rest were made blind to
8   the truth, exactly as it stands written: 'God brought upon them a numbness of spirit; he gave them blind eyes and deaf ears, and so
9   it is still.' Similarly David says:

    'May their table be a snare and a trap,
    Both stumbling-block and retribution!
10   May their eyes be darkened so that they do not see!
    Bow down their back for ever!'

11   I now ask, did their failure mean complete downfall? Far from it! Because they offended, salvation has come to the Gentiles, to
12   stir Israel to emulation. But if their offence means the enrichment of the world, and if their falling-off means the enrichment of the Gentiles, how much more their coming to full strength!
13   But I have something to say to you Gentiles. I am a missionary to the Gentiles, and as such I give all honour to that ministry
14   when I try to stir emulation in the men of my own race, and so to

15 save some of them. For if their rejection has meant the reconcili-
16 ation of the world, what will their acceptance mean? Nothing less
than life from the dead! If the first portion of dough is consecrated, so is the whole lump. If the root is consecrated, so are the
17 branches. But if some of the branches have been lopped off, and
you, a wild olive, have been grafted in among them, and have
18 come to share the same root and sap as the olive, do not make
yourself superior to the branches. If you do so, remember that it
is not you who sustain the root: the root sustains you.

19 You will say, 'Branches were lopped off so that I might be
20 grafted in.' Very well: they were lopped off for lack of faith, and
by faith you hold your place. Put away your pride, and be on
21 your guard; for if God did not spare the native branches, no
22 more will he spare you. Observe the kindness and the severity of
God – severity to those who fell away, divine kindness to you, if
only you remain within its scope; otherwise you too will be cut
23 off, whereas they, if they do not continue faithless, will be grafted
24 in; for it is in God's power to graft them in again. For if you were
cut from your native wild olive and against all nature grafted into
the cultivated olive, how much more readily will they, the natural
olive-branches, be grafted into their native stock!

25 For there is a deep truth here, my brothers, of which I want
you to take account, so that you may not be complacent about
your own discernment: this partial blindness has come upon
Israel only until the Gentiles have been admitted in full strength;
26 when that has happened, the whole of Israel will be saved, in
agreement with the text of Scripture:

> 'From Zion shall come the Deliverer;
> He shall remove wickedness from Jacob.
27 And this is the covenant I will grant them,
> When I take away their sins.'

28 In the spreading of the Gospel they are treated as God's
enemies for your sake; but God's choice stands, and they are his
29 friends for the sake of the patriarchs. For the gracious gifts of
30 God and his calling are irrevocable. Just as formerly you were
disobedient to God, but now have received mercy in the time of
31 their disobedience, so now, when you receive mercy, they have
proved disobedient, but only in order that they too may receive
32 mercy. For in making all mankind prisoners to disobedience,
God's purpose was to show mercy to all mankind.

33 O depth of wealth, wisdom, and knowledge in God! How

127

34 unsearchable his judgements, how untraceable his ways! Who
35 knows the mind of the Lord? Who has been his counsellor? Who
36 has ever made a gift to him, to receive a gift in return? Source,
Guide, and Goal of all that is – to him be glory for ever! Amen.

The chapter is not difficult, read as a whole. I will simply concentrate on particular points of interpretation.

Verses 1–2. The train of the argument is: No, God can't have cast off his people entirely, for I myself am an Israelite. True, the Jews who have become Christians may be a mere handful. But that is no new situation in the history of God's people. Don't you remember what happened in the time of Elijah? (verses 2–4).

Verse 8. 'God brought upon them a numbness of spirit.' This, as everything that Paul has said makes clear, does not mean that they weren't responsible. It means that here was something of more than ordinary human stupidity. The phrase, a Hebraism, probably means not so much 'numbness of spirit' but 'a spirit of (i.e., a superhuman quality of) torpor' – not merely a natural but a praeternatural obtuseness. The biblical way of putting this is to say that God had induced this stupidity. Indeed if there is an ultimate mystery in God's world – and the mystery of why some people accept grace and others don't seems to have little connection with natural goodness – then God must be somewhere behind it. It is when this hardens into a dogma of irresistible grace that human freedom and responsibility disappear; and that never happens in the Bible.

Verses 13–14. This is apparently an interjection, as the argument of verse 15 carries straight on from verse 12. It is to assure the Gentile majority among his readers that he has not been so carried away by his concern for the Jews that he has lost concern for them. On the contrary, the two concerns are linked. So far from soft-pedalling his apostleship to the Gentiles in order to win the Jews, he goes out of his way to magnify that ministry – for that is the best way, he thinks, of saving the Jews; for it will provoke them to emulation. On this Dodd shrewdly comments: 'He certainly did make them jealous, but if he really thought that it would have any such desirable result, he was a great optimist!'

Verses 16–24. The image of the olive-tree, like that of the vine and the fig-tree, is a stock parable for Israel. Cf. Jer. 11.16: 'Once the Lord called you an olive-tree, leafy and fair; but now with a great roaring noise you will feel sharp anguish; fire sets its leaves alight and consumes its branches.'

In the allegory, whose argument is clear enough, Paul is describing something that completely reverses anything that the farmer does. As with other fruit trees or roses, it is a cutting from a cultivated olive that has to be grafted on to the wild stock if the fruit is not to be valueless. Grafting a twig of wild olive into a cultivated tree would be useless. This has been taken to prove that Paul as a townsman had no idea what he was talking about. As Dodd puts it, 'he had not the curiosity to enquire what went on in the olive-yards which fringed every road that he walked'. But seldom, I think, has criticism been more misplaced. For Paul is perfectly aware that the whole process he is describing is 'against all nature' (verse 24) – and the whole force of his argument depends on this. The inclusion of the Gentiles has from beginning to end been a matter not of nature but of grace. So that is why the conclusion can and must run: therefore presume on nothing. Yet in contrast with the parables of Jesus Paul starts from theology not from nature – and this again is why his thought is so much less readily assimilable.

Verses 25–36. At this point argument gives way to vision, to revelation (*mystērion*), as in I Cor. 15.51: 'Behold, I tell you a mystery.' The future of God's plan is disclosed only to the eye of faith.

Two points call for comment:

1. Paul's argument about the merits of the patriarchs (verse 28) seems at first sight to go back on what he said about physical descent from Abraham affording no guarantee (9.6–9). Is not salvation on the basis of physical solidarity coming in again by the back door? No, faith and faith alone remains the principle of salvation: it is only 'if they do not continue faithless' (verse 23) that the Jews will be incorporated. As Sanday and Headlam put

it: 'The merits of the Fathers are not then looked upon as the cause of Israel's salvation, but as a guarantee that Israel will attain that faith which is a necessary condition of their being saved.' But why should it be a guarantee? From two points of view: (*a*) In so far as faith is God's gift, 'the gracious gifts of God and his calling are irrevocable' (verse 29). The divine love which chose the patriarchs is not a mutable or wayward affair. (*b*) In so far as faith is a human response, the zeal for God (10.2) which from Abraham onwards has been part of the life-blood of the Jewish people cannot count for nothing. The root and sap of the olive are not destroyed whatever may happen to the branches (verses 17–18).

But ultimately the argument is not a logical one, and Paul does not claim that it is. As Dodd sums it up: 'The fact is that he has argued from the promise to Abraham on two divergent and perhaps inconsistent lines. If the promise means ultimate blessedness for "Israel", then *either* the historical nation of Israel may be regarded as the heir of the promise (as in 11.28–29), and Paul is justified in saying that "all Israel will be saved", *or* its place may be taken by the New Israel (as in 9.6–8), the Body of Christ in which there is neither Jew nor Greek; but in that case there is no ground for assigning any special place in the future to the Jewish nation as such. Paul tries to have it both ways. We can well understand that his emotional interest in his own people, rather than strict logic, has determined his forecast.' But is it only 'his emotional interest in his own people'? Maybe. But Paul claims that it is grounded in something much more profound, though equally alogical. And we could do worse than sit under his own warning: 'For there is a deep truth here, my brothers, of which I want you to take account, so that you may not be complacent about your own discernment' (verse 25). There is a finely balanced assessment of the issues (as to whether Paul was anti-semitic or too semitic) in W. D. Davies's presidential address to the Society for New Testament Studies in *New Testament Studies*, 24, 1977–8, pp. 4–39. 'Paul's quandary', he says, 'was precisely this: how to do justice to the historical role of his own people without thereby, *ipso facto*, elevating their ethnic character to a position of special privilege'.

2. What does Paul mean or imply by the statements that 'the whole of Israel will be saved' (verse 26) and that God's purpose is 'to show mercy to all mankind' (verse 32)? As far as his immediate meaning is concerned it is clear that his problem throughout these chapters is not with the ultimate destiny of individuals but with the relation of different groups (Israel according to the flesh and the Gentiles) to incorporation into the true Israel, i.e., to the possibility of salvation. All that Paul is actually saying is that no groups as such will ultimately be excluded. He is not saying that every member of those groups, any more than every person already within the Christian church, will in fact ultimately be saved. For he constantly warns that incorporation into Christ is by itself no guarantee against ultimate reprobation, any more than incorporation into Abraham or Moses (cf. I Cor. 10.1–12). Indeed in this very passage he says: 'They were lopped off for lack of faith. ... Be on your guard; for if God did not spare the native branches, no more will he spare you' (verse 20–21). For him there is always the final day of retribution, when God's just judgment will be revealed and men will be divided according to their way of life (2.5–10).

But though Paul is not asserting here the ultimate salvation of every individual, the question can still be asked whether this is not in fact the implication of the boundless and all-embracing sovereignty of the divine love upon which he closes; whether in the last analysis the pattern 'he makes all men prisoners to disobedience, only that he may have mercy on all' does not hold for individuals as well as for groups; whether, in other words, hell can ever be permanent for any; or whether the call to every individual, like the call to Israel, to be a son of God is not equally 'without repentance'. These questions cannot be answered from this passage. They must be considered in the light also of such passages as Col. 1.20, where it is said that in the cross God willed to reconcile to himself all in heaven and earth alike, and Eph. 1.10, where it is said that it was 'the purpose of

131

God's design so to order it in the fulness of the ages that all things in heaven and earth alike should be gathered up in Christ'. The problems involved in the universalist conclusion are enormous and should not be minimized. But to discuss them all (philosophical and exegetical alike) would take us far beyond our present scope. I can only refer again for my own tentative grasp of them to my *In the End God*, chapters 10 and 11. But on the passage in front of us I would concur with Dodd's concluding remarks: 'If Paul believed that such a thorough-going redintegration of the universe was the end of the divine purpose, then he cannot but have thought that a complete redintegration of the human race was included in it; and he may be allowed to have meant what he said in its full sense: that God would "have mercy upon all". If we really believe in One God, and believe that Jesus Christ, in what he was and what he did, truly shows us what God's character and his attitude to men are like, then it is very difficult to think ourselves out of the belief that somehow his love will find a way of bringing all men into unity with him.'

Verses 33–36. There is a fascinating and instructive contrast with the parallel and poignant discussion in the apocalypse of II Esd. 3–9, headed in the NEB 'The mystery of human destiny'. This comes from about AD 100 (cf. 3.1) and reflects the fall of Jerusalem and the desolation of Israel. Ezra asks: 'Why have you humiliated this one stock more than all the others?' God replies: 'You are in great sorrow of heart for Israel's sake. Do you love Israel more than Israel's Maker does?' 'No, my lord', I said, 'but sorrow has forced me to speak; my heart is tortured every hour as I try to understand the ways of the Most High and to fathom some part of his judgments' (5.28–34). The argument goes to and fro with Ezra trying to get God to justify his ways in creating the vast mass of mankind apparently for destruction. He fails to get any satisfying answer, and the dialogue peters out with God saying almost in self-pity through his angel: 'I looked at my world, and there it lay spoilt, at my earth in danger from men's wicked thoughts; and at the sight I could scarcely bring myself to spare them. One grape I saved out of a cluster, one tree out of a forest. So then let it be: destruction for the many who were born in vain, and salvation for my grape and my tree, which have cost me such labour to bring to perfection' (9.20–22). The comparison of that with Rom. 11.23–36 is perhaps the best commentary on the difference that Christ makes.

12.1–21

Christian Behaviour

12 Therefore, my brothers, I implore you by God's mercy to offer your very selves to him: a living sacrifice, dedicated and fit for his
2 acceptance, the worship offered by mind and heart.ᵃ Adapt yourselves no longer to the pattern of this present world, but let your minds be remade and your whole nature thus transformed. Then you will be able to discern the will of God, and to know what is good, acceptable, and perfect.

3 In virtue of the gift that God in his grace has given me I say to everyone among you: do not be conceited or think too highly of yourself; but think your way to a sober estimate based on the
4 measure of faith that God has dealt to each of you. For just as in a single human body there are many limbs and organs, all with
5 different functions, so all of us, united with Christ, form one body, serving individually as limbs and organs to one another.

6 The gifts we possess differ as they are allotted to us by God's
7 grace, and must be exercised accordingly: the gift of administra-
8 tion, in administration. A teacher should employ his gift in teaching, and one who has the gift of stirring speech should use it to stir his hearers. If you give to charity, give with all your heart; if you are a leader, exert yourself to lead; if you are helping others in distress, do it cheerfully.

9 10 Love in all sincerity, loathing evil and clinging to the good. Let love for our brotherhood breed warmth of mutual affection. Give pride of place to one another in esteem.

11 With unflagging energy, in ardour of spirit, serve the Lord.ᵇ
12 Let hope keep you joyful; in trouble stand firm; persist in prayer.

133

13   Contribute to the needs of God's people, and practise hospitality.

14   Call down blessings on your persecutors – blessings, not curses.

15   With the joyful be joyful, and mourn with the mourners.

16   Have equal regard for one another. Do not be haughty, but go about with humble folk. Do not keep thinking how wise you are.

17   Never pay back evil for evil. Let your aims be such as all men
18 count honourable. If possible, so far as it lies with you, live at
19 peace with all men. My dear friends, do not seek revenge, but leave a place for divine retribution; for there is a text which
20 reads, 'Justice is mine, says the Lord, I will repay.' But there is another text: 'If your enemy is hungry, feed him; if he is thirsty, give him a drink; by doing this you will heap live coals on his
21 head.' Do not let evil conquer you, but use good to defeat evil.

a. Or ... acceptance, for such is the worship which you, as rational creatures, should offer.
b. Some witnesses read meet the demands of the hour.

With chapter 12 we return to the conclusion to be drawn – or rather to be lived out – from chapter 8. In 8.3–4 Paul had said: 'What the law could never do ... God has done ..., so that the commandment of the law may find fulfilment in us, whose conduct, no longer ˏunder the control of our lower nature, is directed by the Spirit.' The logic, as always in Christian ethics, is not the Kantian 'You ought, therefore you can' but 'You can, therefore you ought'. Paul now goes on to say what 'the commandment of the law' is for the Christian, and his conclusion is that 'the whole law is summed up in love' (13.10). Put another way, this is an expansion of what he sketched in chapter 6. The righteousness which is given to the Christian is not in the first instance a moral category: it is a standing before God, acceptance by him. But once given it involves a wholly new quality of life which is ethical through and through: 'As once you yielded your bodies to the service of impurity and lawlessness ... so now yield them to the service of righteousness' (6.19). This is what is taken up in 12.1, where the verb he uses is the same.

There are few points that call for comment.

Verse 1. 'A living sacrifice' (*logikēn latreian*): not 'reasonable service' (AV) but worship offered at the level of *logos* and not merely of flesh – what the early church later contrasted with the bloody sacrifices of Jews and pagans; cf. the 'spiritual sacrifices' of I Peter 2.5. For the Stoic background of this phrase, see Barrett.

Verses 4–21. The logic is that of I Cor. 12–13: from the fact of the body of Christ (verses 4–5 = I Cor. 12.12–27) to the diversity of ministry within it (verses 6–8 = I Cor. 12.28–30) to the absolute and overriding requirement of love (verses 9–21 = I Cor. 13).

In the next chapter Paul continues to expound the meaning of this Christian love (*agapē*) in terms of what is 'due' to all men; and he begins with the realm of impersonal institutions where the relevance of the commandment to love is most difficult to see or to apply. The connecting link is in the theme introduced in verse 19, of 'revenge' and 'retribution'.

13.1–14

---

13 Every person must submit to the supreme authorities. There is no authority but by act of God, and the existing authorities are
2 instituted by him; consequently anyone who rebels against authority is resisting a divine institution, and those who so resist have themselves to thank for the punishment they will receive.
3 For government, a terror to crime, has no terrors for good behaviour. You wish to have no fear of the authorities? Then
4 continue to do right and you will have their approval, for they are God's agents working for your good. But if you are doing wrong, then you will have cause to fear them; it is not for nothing that they hold the power of the sword, for they are God's agents of
5 punishment, for retribution on the offender. That is why you are obliged to submit. It is an obligation imposed not merely by fear
6 of retribution but by conscience. That is also why you pay taxes.

The authorities are in God's service and to these duties they devote their energies.

7 Discharge your obligations to all men; pay tax and toll, rever-
8 ence and respect, to those to whom they are due. Leave no claim outstanding against you, except that of mutual love. He who
9 loves his neighbour has satisfied every claim of the law. For the commandments, 'Thou shalt not commit adultery, thou shalt not kill, thou shalt not steal, thou shalt not covet', and any other commandment there may be, are all summed up in the one rule,
10 'Love your neighbour as yourself.' Love cannot wrong a neigh-bour; therefore the whole law is summed up in love.*a*
11 In all this, remember how critical the moment is. It is time for you to wake out of sleep, for deliverance is nearer to us now than
12 it was when first we believed. It is far on in the night; day is near. Let us therefore throw off the deeds of darkness and put on our
13 armour as soldiers of the light. Let us behave with decency as befits the day: no revelling or drunkenness, no debauchery or
14 vice, no quarrels or jealousies! Let Christ Jesus himself be the armour that you wear; give no more thought to satisfying the bodily appetites.

a. Or the whole law is fulfilled by love.

Paul has just said (12.19) that Christians are not to resort to vengeance to try to redress the balance or 'get even' with evil doers, but are to let the forces of restitution and retribution which God has written into the world take their course: 'Give place to "the wrath" ', i.e., of God. He now goes on to speak of one way in which this *orgē* operates, through the divinely ordained order of the state. Here again Christians are to let it take its course and not attempt to go against it. For as an instrument of retribution – which simply means putting back into the moral order what one has taken out – it is a positive source of equilibrium. The state, as Paul insists in II Thess. 2.6–7, is a restraining power, an instrument of God's long-suffering, deferring the sheer chaos of the 'day of wrath' by preserving stability and moral order. (Cf. I Tim. 1.8–9: 'The law is an excellent thing, provided we treat it as law, recognizing that it is not aimed at good citizens, but at the lawless and unruly' – which, whether Paul wrote it or not, is entirely Pauline.) Indeed Christians are not merely not to resist or undermine the power of the state, they are to co-operate with it and submit to it on positive principle ('for conscience sake', verse 5). This directive is partly an extension of his line in 12.17–18 that Christians' aims are to be such as all men recognize as honourable and that as far as lies with them they are to live at peace with all. Let your reputation, Paul is saying, be one of being good citizens and co-operative members of the body politic. This insistence was indeed a matter of critical importance in a situation in which Jews had already been deported from Rome, as Suetonius says, *impulsore Chresto* – because of riots occasioned by Christ, if that is what it means – and which would within a decade lead to Nero fastening on Christians as political scapegoats. It is a directive which is stressed even more urgently in I Peter 3.13–17; 4.12–19.

But for Paul it is much more than a matter of expediency. It is based on his whole theology of the political order. He never purchases his high doctrine of the church at the expense of a low doctrine of the state, any more than he purchases his high doctrine of the ministry at the expense of a low doctrine of the church. (In both these respects F. D. Maurice was in the nineteenth century more truly biblical, and I would say more truly Anglican, than Pusey and most of the Oxford Movement.) In fact Rom. 12.4–13.6 brings all three together, ministry, church and state, in a very interesting way. In a real sense, Paul's doctrines of the church and of the state are parallel, and both have their ministries appointed by God. He employs the same word *diakonos* (minister) of the state in 13.4 as he applies within the church in 12.7; and in 13.6 he uses of the agents of the state the term *leiturgoi* (liturgists), corresponding to the *latreia* or divine service which the church exists to offer (12.1). There is in fact an exact parallel with his own apostolate in 15.16, where he describes himself as a *leiturgos* of Jesus Christ in the priestly service of the gospel, with the Gentiles as the sacrifice he offers. Yet there is also for him an important difference between church and state expressed in the fact that whereas the minister of state is a *leiturgos* of *God*, Paul as a minister of the church is a *leiturgos* of *Christ*. The state does not know God in Christ, but God as he is apart from Christ: it is the instrument of his *orgē*, not the agent of his *agapē*. But that does not make it any the less divine or any the less directed towards 'the good' (verse 3) – when, that is, it is performing its proper function. Paul does not discuss the Christian's relation to a state which becomes apostate, any more than he discusses the Christian's relation to a church which becomes apostate. In each case he would have been the first to acknowledge that this was a possibility. But here he is simply concerned with the positive meaning of the duty to render to Caesar the things that are Caesar's; he does not discuss, as the book of the Revelation does, what is to happen when Caesar usurps the things that are God's.

Moreover, he discusses the Christian's relation to this entirely in terms of submission. That was the only relevant relation of the early Christian to political power. He does not answer for us the much more difficult problems which arise when the Christian's relation to power (in a democracy such as ours) is not simply one of responsibility to but of responsibility for, when he is not only at the receiving end but at the dispensing end. What becomes the relationship of love to justice when the ministers of the *orgē* are themselves Christians, even perhaps ministers of the church? The one thing that is quite certain is that the problem does not disappear when the Christian ethic of love becomes the professed standard of the state. Power and all that goes with it is built into God's universe; it is ordained by him as part of the structure of life (there is a deep-seated connection between *bios*, life, and *bia*, violence), and if Christians don't take responsibility for it others must. The necessity for the state, for coercion and restraint, for *exousia*, authority, remains as a positive divine ordinance within this age. Absolute pacifism, the refusal to touch force of any kind, except as an *ad hoc* minority witness, like total abstinence, is, as Reinhold Niebuhr stressed, heretical. For the view that power *as such* is evil is only another version of the Manichean heresy that matter as such is evil, since all power, as nuclear power reminds us most vividly, is a function of matter.

Before leaving this passage, I should refer to the interpretation put upon it by Cullmann (following Barth) in his *Christ and Time*, 1951, pp. 191–210, and subsequently defended in *The State in the New Testament*, 1957, pp. 93–114. He takes the *exousiai* of verse 1 to be not simply the political authorities but the cosmic powers, to which indeed this language regularly applies in the New Testament, that lie behind and operate through the political order (cf. especially I Cor. 2.8 for the double reference in the 'rulers' who crucified the Lord of glory). His point is that these powers have now been reconciled and harnessed in Christ and are henceforth 'ministers' of God's will rather than working for the opposition. He puts up a strong case, but I have met few who are really convinced by it. Barrett indeed rejects it outright, on the grounds that the state-authorities for Paul are precisely the bulwark *against* the cosmic powers of darkness and of Satan (II Thess. 2.6–10). It is just when the state becomes identified with the demonic forces that it is *not* to be obeyed. There is indeed nothing in Paul to suggest that Christians should subject themselves to the angelic powers – rather the opposite: the angels are subject to Christ (Phil. 2.10; Col. 2.15) and therefore to Christians: 'Are you not aware that we are to judge angels?' (I Cor. 6.3; cf. Col. 2.18,20).

The Christian's ethical attitude to the state has been expressed throughout this discussion in the categories of what is 'due'. But Paul at once goes on (verses 7–10) to say that love cannot in fact be fully comprehended in such categories. As Jesus said in relation to forgiveness, the Christian life is like being involved in an inexhaustible debt. Love may satisfy every claim of the law, but nothing can satisfy the claims of love. And yet Paul is not left sighing or contorting himself or his readers with 'the relevance of an impossible ethical ideal'. His words lead straight into a clarion call to decisive choice (verses 11–14). You may not be able to love 'to the end' (like Jesus in John 13.1), but the *direction* in which love faces is as different from the direction of self-gratification as light is from darkness. Yet a

Christian is not simply faced with a static choice of duty between light and darkness, day and night, as in the Old Testament and Qumran ethic and left to choose life. On the contrary, he knows that the day is coming to him. The Christian life is offer before it is demand: it is Christ, and Christ coming. But not only this: it is Christ come, the present fact of the new man, the redeemed humanity, which a Christian can put on here and now, and which moreover he *has* put on when he was incorporated into that humanity in baptism. Here as always the call of Christian ethics is to become what you are, to put on what you have already put on, to *be* the members of Christ which you are. It is the body of Christ which is the great new reality of the spiritual order. Chapters 12–15 are really only the moral consequences of what Paul says in 12.5: 'So all of us, united with Christ, form one body, serving individually as limbs and organs to one another'.

This too is the theological principle which gives unity and unerring direction to the very ticklish issue of personal relationships discussed in the section that immediately follows, namely, that 'no one of us lives, and equally no one of us dies, for himself alone' (14.7).

14.1–15.6

---

14 If a man is weak in his faith you must accept him without
2 attempting to settle doubtful points. For instance, one man will have faith enough to eat all kinds of food, while a weaker man
3 eats only vegetables. The man who eats must not hold in contempt the man who does not, and he who does not eat must not pass judgement on the one who does; for God has accepted him.
4 Who are you to pass judgement on someone else's servant? Whether he stands or falls is his own Master's business; and he will, because his Master has power to enable him to stand.
5 Again, this man regards one day more highly than another,

while that man regards all days alike. On such a point everyone
6 should have reached conviction in his own mind. He who respects the day has the Lord in mind in doing so, and he who eats meat has the Lord in mind when he eats, since he gives thanks to God; and he who abstains has the Lord in mind no less, since he too gives thanks to God.

7 For no one of us lives, and equally no one of us dies, for
8 himself alone. If we live, we live for the Lord; and if we die, we die for the Lord. Whether therefore we live or die, we belong to
9 the Lord. This is why Christ died and came to life again, to
10 establish his lordship over dead and living. You, sir, why do you pass judgement on your brother? And you, sir, why do you hold your brother in contempt? We shall all stand before God's tri-
11 bunal. For Scripture says, 'As I live, says the Lord, to me every
12 knee shall bow and every tongue acknowledge God.' So, you see, each of us will have to answer for himself.

13 Let us therefore cease judging one another, but rather make this simple judgement: that no obstacle or stumbling-block be
14 placed in a brother's way. I am absolutely convinced, as a Christ-ian, that nothing is impure in itself; only if a man considers a
15 particular thing impure, then to him it is impure. If your brother is outraged by what you eat, then your conduct is no longer
16 guided by love. Do not by your eating bring disaster to a man for whom Christ died! What for you is a good thing must not become
17 an occasion for slanderous talk; for the kingdom of God is not eating and drinking, but justice, peace, and joy, inspired by the
18 Holy Spirit. He who thus shows himself a servant of Christ is acceptable to God and approved by men.

19 Let us then pursue the things that make for peace and build up
20 the common life. Do not ruin the work of God for the sake of food. Everything is pure in itself, but anything is bad for the man
21 who by his eating causes another to fall. It is a fine thing to abstain from eating meat or drinking wine, or doing anything
22 which causes your brother's downfall. If you have a clear convic-tion, apply it to yourself in the sight of God. Happy is the man
23 who can make his decision with a clear conscience![a] But a man who has doubts is guilty if he eats, because his action does not arise from his conviction, and anything which does not arise from
15 conviction is sin. Those of us who have a robust conscience must accept as our own burden the tender scruples of weaker men,
2 and not consider ourselves. Each of us must consider his neigh-bour and think what is for his good and will build up the common

141

3   life. For Christ too did not consider himself, but might have said,
     in the words of Scripture, 'The reproaches of those who
4   reproached thee fell upon me.' For all the ancient scriptures were
     written for our own instruction, in order that through the
     encouragement they give us we may maintain our hope with
5   fortitude. And may God, the source of all fortitude and all
     encouragement, grant that you may agree with one another after
6   the manner of Christ Jesus, so that with one mind and one voice
     you may praise the God and Father of our Lord Jesus Christ.

a Or who does not bring judgement upon himself by what he approves!

This is the sort of issue that reveals Paul at his clearest and
surest. You feel he knows exactly where to put his finger. His
argument has an intellectual and moral directness which makes
commentary unnecessary – though for a most illuminating and
suggestive discussion of it in the light of modern parallels, and
with reference to modern situations which are *not* parallel, see
Dodd, who is also here at his surest.

Note only the theological foundations to which Paul appeals
for his ethical conclusions. (1) There is first and all through the
appeal to the fact of the body of Christ, to which we have
already referred, and which the phrase 'in the Lord Jesus' in
14.14 (NEB 'as a Christian') and the word *oikodomē*, 'building
up' in 14.19 and 15.2 implicitly presuppose. (2) But there is also
in 14.3 ('He who does not eat meat must not pass judgement on
the one who does; for God has *accepted* him') the basic principle of justification by faith: 'You are accepted'. It is the same
appeal to the divine *charis* or generosity which Jesus made the
basis of the moral response (Luke 6.32–36). (3) There is in 14.4
('his Master has power to enable him to stand') the appeal not
only to final judgment (as in verse 10) but to the ultimate saving
power of God. (4) There is the appeal *en passant* to the great
saving acts of the passion, death and resurrection of Christ in
15.3; 14.15 and 14.9 – so typical of Paul in ethical contexts (the
locus classicus being Phil. 2.5–11). (5) Finally, there is the rare
allusion to the kingdom of God (14.17), which here, as Black
says, is the equivalent of the *regula dei*, as in the Rabbinic

commonplace of taking upon oneself the 'yoke' of the kingship of God. It should be translated: 'Living by God's rule' does not mean observing food-laws but pursuing justice, peace, etc. Note also in 14.20 the unique phrase 'the work of God', for which the only parallel is the expression 'the Father's work' in John 17.4, etc., for the whole act of God in Christ. (Our phrase 'the work of Christ' does not in fact occur in the Bible.)

Even where Paul is being most practical and pastoral, there he is most theological. His appeal is not to moral generalities like broadmindedness and tolerance, but to the very heart of what God has done and has given us in Jesus Christ. It is because his principles are so theological that his touch is so unerring. The church neglects theology at the risk of losing all cutting edge and being reduced to moralizing!

15.7–13

---

7 In a word, accept one another as Christ accepted us, to the glory
8 of God. I mean that Christ became a servant of the Jewish people to maintain the truth of God by making good his promises to the
9 patriarchs, and at the same time to give the Gentiles cause to glorify God for his mercy. As Scripture says, 'Therefore I will
10 praise thee among the Gentiles and sing hymns to thy name'; and
11 again, 'Gentiles, make merry together with his own people'; and yet again, 'All Gentiles, praise the Lord; let all peoples praise
12 him.' Once again, Isaiah says, 'There shall be the Root of Jesse, the one raised up to govern the Gentiles; on him the Gentiles
13 shall set their hope.' And may the God of hope fill you with all joy and peace by your faith in him, until, by the power of the Holy Spirit, you overflow with hope.

The function of this paragraph (the final 'lock' in the canal) is to draw all the threads of the epistle together. The last discussion may seem to have taken us a long way from the rarified heights of chapters 1–8. Yet it is simply the gospel of justification by faith in the imperative. Moreover, this tension between those who observed food-laws and sabbath-days and those who didn't was only, as Paul has hitherto tactfully refrained from rubbing in, the old antagonism of Jew and Gentile. (For Paul, the Jew is always the weaker brother, as in the closely parallel discussion in I Cor. 8–10.) And it was precisely in the breaking down of this barrier once and for all that for him the gospel consisted: 'Accept one another as Christ has accepted us (both Jew and Gentile), to the glory of God' (verse 7). This is the explicit and controlling theme of Ephesians, but the whole drift of Rom. 1–11 has been to show that Christ made himself *both* the 'servant of the Jewish people to maintain the truth of God by making good his promises to the patriarchs' *and* at the same time the bringer of God's 'mercy' to the Gentiles (verses 8–9). But once more Paul cannot leave the theme without appeal to scripture (verses 9–12), and again to his favourite sources, Deuteronomy, the Psalms and Isaiah – showing thereby, as Dodd says, not only that it was so but that it must have been so. And again the emphasis is laid on the side that seemed most incredible, that the Gentiles could really be within the divine scope and promised hope. For previously, as he rubs in in Eph. 2.12, they were absolutely outside the Christ, aliens from the commonwealth of Israel, strangers to the covenants of promise: their world was a world without hope and without God.

Finally, the benediction (verse 13) gathers up all the key words of chapters 1–8: faith, hope, joy, peace and the power of the Holy Spirit.

Dodd sums it all up in words that cannot be bettered: 'The great argument is ended. Paul set out to lay before the Roman church the "Gospel" which he was eager to preach in Rome, because he was "proud of it" as being "God's saving power". He has shown them how "God's righteousness is revealed in it", by justifying sinful men on the ground of faith alone, and by saving them from the power of sin into a life of the Spirit. He has shown how, though this "righteousness" was promised first to Israel, the promise rightly includes the Gentiles in its scope, and will ultimately be fulfilled for all men. Finally, he has shown them that though the Gospel supersedes the Jewish Law, yet it does not fall away from the moral demands for which the Law stood, but creates its own new morality, which is "God's righteousness" at work in human lives, because it is rooted in divine love. That is his Gospel. The Romans must judge of it. It remains only to speak of some personal matters.'

These personal matters in so far as they require comment have already engaged our attention at the beginning, so they can be left to speak for themselves.

15.14–16.23

14 My friends, I have no doubt in my mind that you yourselves are quite full of goodness and equipped with knowledge of every
15 kind, well able to give advice to one another; nevertheless I have written to refresh your memory, and written somewhat boldly at
16 times, in virtue of the gift I have from God. His grace has made me a minister of Christ Jesus to the Gentiles; my priestly service is the preaching of the gospel of God, and it falls to me to offer the Gentiles to him as[a] an acceptable sacrifice, consecrated by the Holy Spirit.
17 Thus in the fellowship of Christ Jesus I have ground for pride
18 in the service of God. I will venture to speak of those things alone in which I have been Christ's instrument to bring the Gen-
19 tiles into his allegiance, by word and deed, by the force of miraculous signs and by the power of the Holy Spirit. As a result I have completed the preaching of the gospel of Christ from
20 Jerusalem as far round as Illyricum. It is my ambition to bring the gospel to places where the very name of Christ has not been heard, for I do not want to build on another man's foundation;
21 but, as Scripture says,

> 'They who had no news of him shall see,
> And they who never heard of him shall understand.'

22 That is why I have been prevented all this time from coming to

145

23 you. But now I have no further scope in these parts, and I have
24 been longing for many years to visit you on my way to Spain; for
I hope to see you as I travel through, and to be sent there with
25 your support after having enjoyed your company for a while. But
at the moment I am on my way to Jerusalem, on an errand to
26 God's people there. For Macedonia and Achaia have resolved to
raise a common fund for the benefit of the poor among God's
27 people at Jerusalem. They have resolved to do so, and indeed
they are under an obligation to them. For if the Jewish Christians
shared their spiritual treasures with the Gentiles, the Gentiles
28 have a clear duty to contribute to their material needs. So when I
have finished this business and delivered the proceeds under my
29 own seal, I shall set out for Spain by way of your city, and I am
sure that when I arrive I shall come to you with a full measure of
the blessing of Christ.

30 I implore you by our Lord Jesus Christ and by the love that the
31 Spirit inspires, be my allies in the fight; pray to God for me that I
may be saved from unbelievers in Judaea and that my errand to
32 Jerusalem may find acceptance with God's people, so that by his
will I may come to you in a happy frame of mind and enjoy a
33 time of rest with you. The God of peace be with you all. Amen.

16 I commend to you Phoebe, a fellow-Christian who holds office in
2 the congregation at Cenchreae. Give her, in the fellowship of
Christ, a welcome worthy of God's people, and stand by her in
any business in which she may need your help, for she has herself
been a good friend to many, including myself.

3 Give my greetings to Prisca and Aquila, my fellow-workers in
4 Christ. They risked their necks to save my life, and not I alone
5 but all the gentile congregations are grateful to them. Greet also
the congregation at their house.

Give my greetings to my dear friend Epaenetus, the first con-
6 vert to Christ in Asia, and to Mary, who toiled hard for you.
7 Greet Andronicus and Junias[b] my fellow-countrymen and com-
rades in captivity. They are eminent among the apostles, and
they were Christians before I was.

8 Greetings to Ampliatus, my dear friend in the fellowship of the
9 Lord, to Urban my comrade in Christ, and to my dear Stachys.
10 My greetings to Apelles, well proved in Christ's service, to the
11 household of Aristobulus, and my countryman Herodion, and to
those of the household of Narcissus who are in the Lord's fellow-
12 ship. Greet Tryphaena and Tryphosa, who toil in the Lord's

service, and dear Persis who has toiled in his service so long.
13 Give my greetings to Rufus, an outstanding follower of the Lord,
14 and to his mother, whom I call mother too. Greet Asyncritus, Phlegon, Hermes, Patrobas, Hermas, and all friends in their
15 company. Greet Philologus and Julia;*c* Nereus and his sister, and Olympas, and all God's people associated with them.
16 Greet one another with the kiss of peace. All Christ's congregations send you their greetings.
17 I implore you, my friends, keep your eyes on those who stir up quarrels and lead others astray, contrary to the teaching you
18 received. Avoid them, for such people are servants not of Christ our Lord but of their own appetites, and they seduce the minds
19 of innocent people with smooth and specious words. The fame of your obedience has spread everywhere. This makes me happy about you; yet I should wish you to be experts in goodness but
20 simpletons in evil; and the God of peace will soon crush Satan beneath your feet. The grace of our Lord Jesus be with you!*d*
21 Greetings to you from my colleague Timothy, and from
22 Lucius, Jason, and Sosipater my fellow-countrymen. (I Tertius,
23 who took this letter down, add my Christian greetings.) Greetings also from Gaius, my host and host of the whole congregation, and from Erastus, treasurer of this city, and our brother Quartus.*e*

a. *Or* ...of God, so that the worship which the Gentiles offer may be ...
b. *Or* Junia; *some ancient witnesses read* Julia, *or* Julias.
c. *Or* Julias; *some witnesses read* Junia, *or* Junias.
d. *The words* The grace ... with you *are omitted at this point in some witnesses; in some, these or similar words are given as verse 24, and in some others after verse 27 (see note on verse 23).*
e. *Some witnesses add* (24) The grace of our Lord Jesus Christ be with you all!

16.25–27

Finally, we come to the doxology, which may not be Paul's own, but as it stands as a fitting comment on the grand theme of his greatest epistle, so let it serve as the gloria for what we too have learnt of him.

25 To him who has power to make your standing sure, according to the Gospel I brought you and the proclamation of Jesus Christ, according to the revelation of that divine secret kept in silence

26 for long ages but now disclosed, and through prophetic scriptures by eternal God's command made known to all nations, to bring

27 them to faith and obedience – to God who alone is wise, through Jesus Christ,*a* be glory for endless ages! Amen.*b,c*

a. Some witnesses insert to whom.
b. Here some witnesses add The grace of our Lord Jesus Christ be with you!
c. Some witnesses place verses 25–27 at the end of chapter 14, one other places them at the end of chapter 15, and others omit them altogether.